PRESENTING
NOW

PRESENTING
NOW

A Guide to Public Speaking and Leadership Communication Online, in Person, and Beyond

SPOKEN WITH AUTHORITY

CHRISTINE CLAPP AND BJØRN F. STILLION SOUTHARD

Presenting Now: A Guide to Public Speaking and Leadership Communication Online, in Person, and Beyond by Christine Clapp and Bjørn F. Stillion Southard

Published by Spoken with Authority®, 326 11th St. NE, Washington, DC 20002
www.spokenwithauthority.com

Library of Congress Control Number: 2022914234

ISBN: 979-8-9863118-0-7 (print)
ISBN: 979-8-9863118-1-4 (ebook)

Cover Photo: Licensed Adobe Stock Image #476387900
Editor: Laurie Weisler
Cover Design and Interior Formatting: Becky's Graphic Design® LLC

Printed in the United States of America
First Edition

To our debate coach Robert Trapp.

Thank you for partnering us in 1998 and setting this all in motion.

Contents

Speaking Roles

INTRODUCTION

Biological evolution can take millennia. Changes in the professional world seem to move at a similar, glacial pace. It took a once-in-a-century pandemic to shift work and workplace communication in dramatic ways. Offices dispersed; face-to-face became face-to-screen; work that previously could (supposedly) never be done online was moved online; and work that truly is best done in person was moved to a virtual platform. Everything moved online, including meetings, presentations, conferences, conversations, and even celebrations. The changes came fast, and we all did our best to keep up.

However, flying by the seat of your pants is not a viable long-term strategy. That is why in June 2020, we published an e-book titled *Presenting Virtually: A Guide to Public Speaking in Professional Contexts*. This e-book adapted principles from our 2016 book *Presenting at Work: A Guide to Public Speaking in Professional Contexts* to respond to online communication and the dramatic shift to work from home.

We have seen more shifts in work and workplace communication since the publication of *Presenting Virtually* a few years ago. Some organizations and sectors have returned to their pre-pandemic norms while others have redefined their version of business as usual as a fully remote experience. Whether your workplace is situated at one end of this spectrum or somewhere in between, we think that Dr. Anthony Fauci had it right in spring 2020 when COVID-19 vaccines were becoming more widely available. He told optimistic Americans there would be no returning to "normal" from the coronavirus pandemic.[1] His forecast was fitting for the pandemic's impact on workplace communication too. After all, technology-mediated communication will forever be a part of the business landscape and in-person communication will never be quite the same either.

> *Technology-mediated communication will forever be a part of the business landscape and in-person communication will never be quite the same either.*

It may be difficult to say goodbye to pre-pandemic norms of work and workplace communication, but like any yearning for halcyon days of the past, there are many problems and injustices that can be glossed over when we glorify the past. Pre-pandemic expectations for universal work at the office made life more difficult for people with disabilities, neurodivergent individuals, caregivers, commuters, introverts, and others. It was worse for the environment; expectations about "professional" hairstyles, clothes, and communication were not inclusive; and many professionals were resistant to trying new and exciting technologies to connect and engage, and had become comfortable with outmoded, time and resource intensive, and exclusionary patterns of in-person communication. We now have an extraordinary opportunity to reinvent post-pandemic communication, both online and in person, in ways that are more flexible, authentic, engaging, equitable, and sustainable.

> *We have an extraordinary opportunity to reinvent post-pandemic communication, both online and in person, in ways that are more flexible, authentic, engaging, equitable, and sustainable.*

Presenting Now helps professionals do just that—become nimble, effective presenters. It offers foundational information on creating and delivering messages that effectively connect with audiences. It builds on lessons learned since early 2020 and takes into account where and how presentations are happening now.

To those ends, we have divided the text into three sections. Part I addresses Content. This section of the book offers useful strategies for analyzing your audience and tools for structuring your content in a clear, concise, and compelling way that is appropriate to the situation. Part II covers Delivery. This section addresses issues related to delivering your message confidently and authentically—whether you are online or in person. Part III discusses Speaking Roles. This section focuses on how to successfully navigate a variety of speaking roles and situations you may encounter in the professional world.

The chapters contained within these three sections are concisely presented, providing actionable information and exercises. We have chosen to limit theoretical discussions within the text, including it only where applicable and providing an occasional footnote for those who are interested in pursuing certain topics more deeply. Each chapter stands on its own—you need not read it cover to cover to glean useful insights. We want the information to be easily accessible and digestible, and helpful at multiple stages of your professional development.

Presenting Now will help you navigate the process of presenting now, whether in a face-to-face pitch, an online interview, a hybrid department meeting, a virtual conference, or any of the other speaking contexts that professionals find themselves in today. Most importantly, we believe that the tools and advice provided in this book will allow you to adapt new presentations in new contexts. Adaptation—thoughtful, meaningful, purposeful, adaptation—has never been more important.

QUICK START GUIDE

This book need not be read cover-to-cover. Each chapter stands on its own, and with a small investment of time can help you enhance a specific presentation skill or prepare for a specific speaking role. To get acquainted with foundational concepts and the most often used tools and approaches in this book, we recommend that you start by reading:

- Chapter 2 on *Nervousness and Confidence*
- Chapter 5 on *The Sandwich Structure*
- Chapter 10 on *The Six Elements of Executive Presence and Authenticity*

Notes:

1. "US May Never Get Back to 'Normal' After Coronavirus Crisis, Dr. Anthony Fauci Says," *Today*, April 7, 2020, https://www.today.com/health/dr-anthony-fauci-us-may-never-get-back-normal-after-t177799

Chapter 1

ETHICS AND INCLUSION

Public speaking instruction has been concerned with ethics since the philosophers Plato and Aristotle founded and shaped the discipline of rhetoric in ancient Greece. A particularly useful definition of an ethical orator comes from the preface of the Roman rhetorician Quintilian's twelve-volume textbook *Institutio Oratoria* written around 95 AD. He wrote in the preface, "My aim, then, is the education of the perfect orator. The first essential for such a one is that he should be a good man, and consequently we demand of him not merely the possession of exceptional gifts of speech, but of all the excellences of character as well."[1]

What insights does this two-thousand-year-old definition of ethics offer today? After all, orators are now women and people of all gender identities, sexual orientations, cultures, races, religions, ages, and abilities. Speakers now have access to the Internet, smartphones, videoconference platforms, virtual reality, and other technologies. They speak in boardrooms, at conferences, on TED stages, with FaceTime, in the Metaverse, via social media, and in situations unfathomable to Quintilian. They are faced with questions about when it is necessary to cite a source in a speech to avoid accusations of academic dishonesty or plagiarism; how to respond when asked to moderate a panel of experts who all identify as white males; and what to do when conference planners hold an organization's annual conference in person after several years online during the pandemic without any virtual options for attendees who feel safer or find it easier to attend virtually due to health concerns, caregiving responsibilities, disability status, or travel costs.

These scenarios represent the difficulty of talking about ethics in presenting. Ethics, like so much of public speaking, is about the relationship between a speaker, the message, and the audience—exactly what Quintilian was getting at two millennia ago with his definition of the "perfect orator." The guiding principle of speaking ethically is not to be perfect but to respect vigilantly the three elements of the presentation: your message, your audience, and yourself. Here's how to do so with a heightened sense of awareness.

Vigilantly Respect Your Message

Respecting the message requires that content be accurate and inclusive. Accuracy includes verifying supporting material that you found in a second-hand account, checking the veracity of claims made by others that you intend to use in your presentation, avoiding the use of statistics that may be helpful to your argument but that are inconsistent with the bulk of research on the topic, making sure that facts and anecdotes are not taken out of context, and following copyright law for media used in your presentation.

> *Respecting the message requires that content be accurate and inclusive.*

Ethical speakers do not plagiarize—intentionally or unintentionally using another person's words or ideas without attribution. There is broad consensus that speakers should never pass off the material of others as their own. However, the situation becomes murky when we need to decide what material speakers should cite in their speeches and how they should be cited.

Though the president may not cite material in speeches, journalists and fact-checking websites make it their job to verify the facts presented. For most speakers, however, presentations are not scrutinized to this degree. For this reason, it is helpful to provide thorough oral citations and even useful descriptions about the authors and publications cited. Such due diligence serves to enhance your credibility. If you are unfamiliar with the expectations of your audience, err on the side of caution and give credit to your sources aloud.

To cite a source in your presentation, include the name of the author, the publication, and the publication date. It is respectful to provide introductory phrases that give listeners context about the author's credentials, the publication's pedigree, and the type of publication if such information would be unfamiliar to an informed audience member. For example, you might say, "in her *New York Times* bestselling memoir *Becoming*, published in 2018, former First Lady Michelle Obama offers a glimpse of life after the White House, 'in this new place, with a lot I want to say.'"[2]

This may seem like a lot of information to say aloud, and it is but for good reason. Audience members do not have the luxury of flipping through a printed works cited or bibliography to locate a source mentioned in your speech. As such, at the time you introduce specific information in your speech, you need to provide enough information for listeners to find the source material on their own, without an undue amount of searching.

Virtual presentations offer the unique opportunity to share links to sources in the chat box or even share entire files, depending on the platform and settings. Consider utilizing these tools to bolster your credibility and make it easier for listeners to access material you cite.

In addition to avoiding plagiarism and crafting accurate content, ethical speakers should take pains to be inclusive. They should reject content and sources that exacerbate or normalize racism, sexism, classism, homophobia, transphobia, and other forms of bigotry. This could mean citing a diverse range of experts and examples, avoiding gender-specific and gender-binary language, and recognizing and responding to implicit biases. Speakers should also craft material that can be experienced by all listeners (more information on presentation aids in chapter 9 and sound in chapter 12).

Vigilantly Respect Your Audience

Respecting your audience begins with topic selection. For starters, remember that presentations are about your audience and not you. This can be especially difficult to remember during technology-mediated communication when your listeners are not in the same room, and even more challenging if you can't even see them on your screen.

> *Remember that presentations are about your audience and not you.*

Frame your topic in terms of the value you can provide the audience based on their needs and interests, not in terms of what you want to talk about. In other words, make it about them (the audience), not you (the speaker). As the speaker, you need to also remember to identify with audience members and not pander to them. Manipulating speech elements in a way that compromises the integrity of the message for the sole purpose of currying the favor of the audience fails to respect the message, audience, and speaker.

Next, you should never be dishonest about your intentions for speaking. If you offer a free educational webinar, do not skimp on substantive content and turn the session into an opportunity to "sell from the lectern." Listeners will feel duped. Instead, provide valuable information to listeners during your webinar without pushing products. This practice builds trust and goodwill with audience members who in turn are more likely to purchase your goods or services in the future.

When determining how much material to include, less is more. Be honest with yourself about need-to-know information versus nice-to-know information. Include the former and cut the latter. When determining how long your remarks will be, take a cue from TED Talks, which are enormously popular and no longer than 18 minutes. In that vein, we recommend that speakers finish their in-person presentation or have a notable change in modality (new speaker, activity, poll, video clip, Q&A, etc.) every 15 to 20 minutes. In a technology-mediated format, we recommend changing modality every five to seven minutes because online attendees have more distractions to contend with.

Regardless of format, keep presentations short. If you are slated to speak for an hour, present for approximately 20 minutes, take questions or otherwise engage audience members for 35 minutes, and save a few minutes for your review, conclusion, and any call to action. You may need to push back on event organizers who give you an unreasonable length of time to speak.

After you craft your content, allot adequate time to rehearse. Delivering an under-prepared or under-rehearsed presentation reflects poorly on the speaker and is disrespectful to listeners. Don't waste the time of audience members by giving a half-baked speech.

> *Delivering an under-prepared or under-rehearsed presentation reflects poorly on the speaker and is disrespectful to listeners.*

How many times, then, do you need to rehearse to be effective? Aim to practice a presentation at least six times before delivering it, as this is the point at which most speakers will become more fluent with content and can present with a more dynamic delivery style. For a more formal speech (such as a keynote address, conference presentation, or TED-style Talk), that number will increase. (See chapter 17 for more on rehearsals.)

During rehearsals, use a stopwatch to check if your presentation meets time constraints. You don't want to insult listeners and event organizers by taking more time than you are allotted or take more time than audience members can be expected to remain attentive. Remember, most speakers prepare more material than they have time to deliver. Always pare down content and practice concise ways of making points; never speak faster to fit it all into the time limits.

Regarding respecting audience members, comply with the Americans with Disabilities Act (ADA) and follow the Web Content Accessibility Guidelines (WCAG) developed by the World Wide Web Consortium (W3C). For presentations in physical settings, this could mean selecting an ADA-compliant location and stage, having sign-language interpretation or assistive-listening systems, including pronouns on name badges, as well as asking attendees ahead of time about food allergies and dietary requirements and providing food items that meet their needs. For virtual presentations, which offer many accessibility advantages, make sure that live captioning is available, allow attendees to add and display pronouns on the web conferencing profile, and use a platform that is screen-reader friendly. Do not require participants to join with their video on; they may not have adequate Internet bandwidth or feel comfortable on camera. If your goal is to promote community or ensure engagement, there are many other tools and strategies to achieve this aim without video.

Announce presentations and meetings times in advance and proactively ask attendees about needed accommodations. Advance notice is necessary to book interpreters and translators, and plan other accommodations. Also, submit presentation materials early so they can be shared ahead of time with interpreters/translators and produced in large print or Braille as needed. Use large print (at least 22-point font) on slides. Use dark text against a light background color. Remember to describe meaningful visuals (what the graph or image looks like or how many people raise their hands to respond to a question), face listeners when speaking (for lip readers), use a high-quality microphone (for amplification and assistive-listening systems), speak at a normal rate with pauses (so interpreters and translators can keep up), and repeat questions from the audience (so everyone can understand).

You can also show respect to audience members after a presentation by seeking feedback. When appropriate, use questionnaires to solicit responses from listeners. To increase response rates, make it easy for survey participants. For in-person presentations, provide a paper evaluation or display a QR code, which is an optical label readable by a camera on a smartphone or tablet that contains information such as a link to your online survey. For online speaking roles, display a QR code on a slide or link to the online survey in the chat box. Consider offering time at the end of your presentation for attendees to respond to the survey—they are much more likely to comply during your session than after it on their own time. In cases where it would be inappropriate or impractical to offer a feedback form or online evaluation, ask key listeners (such as a supervisor or event organizer) for their suggestions on how you can make improvements. Then, analyze the feedback and take steps to incorporate the good advice into future presentations.

Vigilantly Respect Yourself

In as much as a speaker might be a good, ethical person, audience members generally gauge the ethics of a speaker through their presentation. This does not mean that a speaker must elaborate extensively to get across that they are an ethical person. Rather, the character of the speaker is created by the care taken in the composition and delivery of their message. To accept a speaking role on a topic outside your area of expertise or to become sloppy in preparing and presenting can hurt your credibility. Respect yourself enough to decline a speaking role and suggest an alternative speaker if you are unable to provide the time or expertise to do the presentation justice. It is difficult to earn back an audience's trust. It is far better not to lose it in the first place.

> *It is difficult to earn back an audience's trust; it is better not to lose it in the first place.*

Vigilantly respecting your message, audience, and self requires effort. In challenging moments, difficult decisions are often necessary. Following are two examples where speakers grappled with the ethics of their situation. One example comes from Texas high school senior Paxton Smith. She was selected as the commencement speaker for her high school's graduating class. The school administration approved her speech. But at the graduation ceremony on June 2, 2021, Smith made the decision to deliver a different speech, one that focused on the rights of women to control their bodies. It is clear that Smith believed that she must speak out in the face of a new law in Texas that restricted women's access to safe abortions. That new speech vigilantly respected herself and her message. Undoubtedly, some in her audience found her speech inappropriate, offensive, or unethical. The fact that the administration must screen and approve the message suggests that Smith knew that delivering a different speech would at the very least upset the school's administrators. Still, as she told CNN, "It was the right thing to do."[3]

Another example occurred during the 2016 presidential primaries and a September 2015 speech given by U.S. Senator and then presidential candidate Bernie Sanders. Sanders, a Vermont Democrat and not an active member of any religious group, was invited to speak at the staunchly conservative Liberty University in Lynchburg, Virginia. Sanders did not agree with many of the political and social positions that define the school and its leadership.

It would have been unethical for liberal Sanders to pander to the conservative audience when his own beliefs differed. However, Sanders opted to be open and honest about the differences from the outset of his presentation. With the differences expressed directly and swiftly, Sanders proceeded to argue for how he and the audience could reconcile these differences.

Sanders's example shows how a speaker can respect the identity of the audience without pandering, find a way to identify with even the staunchest of critics, and maintain his or her character and credibility when faced with an oppositional audience. As is the case with most questions of ethical public speaking, there isn't a clear-cut formula to "get it right." However, most answers to ethical public speaking questions will involve the same strategy used by Sanders, namely a heightened sense of awareness, thorough preparation, and a dose of courage in order to execute the feat. In order to present ethically, speakers should follow a similar approach by vigilantly respecting their message, their audience, and themselves.

USE LANGUAGE ETHICALLY

Maintaining high ethical standards extends even to the words a speaker chooses. Make the effort to avoid language that denigrates or is hurtful to non-dominant groups and identities, such as women, members of the LGBTQ+ community, or those with disabilities.

Avoid gender stereotyping by using pronouns and terms that are gender inclusive. For example, "A surgeon works long hours; he or she should expect to log at least 80 hours a week during residency." A less wordy and more inclusive construction is the singular use of they/their/ theirs: "A surgeon works long hours; they should expect to log at least 80 hours a week during residency." (Note, in 2017, the Associated Press Stylebook did recognize they as a singular, gender-neutral pronoun.)

Some additional examples are:

AVOID GENDER SPECIFIC	USE GENDER INCLUSIVE
Fireman	Firefighter
Stewardess	Flight attendant
Workman	Worker
Forefathers	Forebears
You guys	You all
Ladies and gentleman	Friends at XYZ organization

Never equate sexuality or intellectual disabilities with something that is undesirable or bad. Never trivialize mental illness.

For example:

AVOID INSENSITIVE	USE INSTEAD
"That movie was gay."	"That movie was terrible."
"That person is crazy."	"That person is acting erratically."
"That's a retarded idea."	"That's a bad idea."

Harvard University and the Linguistic Society of America offer many more insights on how to be more inclusive in your language use.

Notes:

1. Quintilian, *Institutio Oratoria*, Book 1, trans. Harold Edgeworth Butler. Accessed March 10, 2022, http://data.perseus.org/citations/urn:cts:latinLit:phi1002.phi0011.perseus-eng1:pr.

2. Michelle Obama, *Becoming* (New York: Crown Publishing Group, 2018), xix.

3. "'This Was the Right Thing to Do': Valedictorian on Graduation Speech," *CNN*, June 7, 2021, https://cnn.it/3CbXGjf

Chapter 2

NERVOUSNESS AND CONFIDENCE

Perhaps you have heard pronouncements about public speaking and nervousness, such as, "Public speaking is the number one fear among Americans," and "Most people would rather die than give a speech." These overgeneralizations are likely derived from the famous 1973 survey by R.H. Bruskin Associates. It found that of 2,543 American men and women, the fear of public speaking ranked higher than their fear of heights, insects and bugs, and even death.[1]

Am I the Only One?

More recent studies confirm that the fear of public speaking, also known as communication apprehension, communication anxiety, communication avoidance, and glossophobia, are common. A 2017 survey of over 1100 college students found that almost 64 percent reported fear of public speaking.[2] Perhaps that number is low. Mark Twain once famously said, "There are two types of speakers: those that are nervous and those that are liars."

Less typical is social anxiety disorder, where fear can lead to avoidance that disrupts your life. A 1999 study found that 15 percent of Swedish adults had a social phobia and that public speaking was the most common among them.[3] However, Dr. Jeffrey R. Strawn, director of the Anxiety Disorders Research Program in the Department of Psychiatry & Behavioral Neuroscience at the University of Cincinnati, says, "[I]t is important to point out that not all individuals with a fear of public speaking have social anxiety disorder or another psychiatric disorder."[4]

Why Do I Get Nervous?

Researchers theorize that the fear of public speaking likely stems from human survival instincts. After all, in early human history, if eyes were trained on you, you were at risk of becoming a predator's next meal. Today, having colleagues stare at you during a meeting or on a stage at a conference still can trigger the fight-or-flight response.

Dr. Glenn Croston explained in *Psychology Today* another evolutionary reason why public speaking causes panic: "Early humans survived by their wits and their ability to collaborate. Those that worked together well, helping others in their group, probably survived and passed on traits that contributed to social behavior. Failure to be a part of the social group, or getting kicked out, probably spelled doom for early humans. Anything that threatens our status in our social group, like the threat of ostracism, feels like a very great risk to us."[5] For our distant ancestors, articulating an unpopular position meant possible banishment—a prehistoric death sentence.

Today, when you are called on to share your perspective in a call with clients, on a panel of experts, or during a presentation at a conference, your amygdala—the part of the brain that regulates fear—still reads the situation as life and death (even though it is not). Your body has an instinctive reaction to the perceived threat and instinctively goes into fight-or-flight mode by releasing hormones that give you a boost of energy. That neural response can cause symptoms of nervousness, such as increased heart or breathing rate, increased sweating, flushing, dry mouth, stiffness in the muscles of the back or neck, nausea, dizziness, or even panic.

What Should I Do About Nervousness?

Talk to Your Doctor

If you find yourself avoiding public speaking or experiencing new or worsening symptoms when you do, you should request a screening for a social anxiety disorder by your primary-care provider or mental-health practitioner. Chances are, you don't have one, but it's similar to when you have pain in your knee—you need to get it checked out by an orthopedist before starting a physical therapy regimen to rule out any breaks or tears that need immediate intervention before rehabilitation. It is crucial to rule out or get treated for social anxiety disorder before continuing with any presentations-skills training or coaching regimen to ensure you are being productive and not causing psychological harm.

Accept Nervousness

If you are like many Americans who fear public speaking, or if you are part of the smaller number who have a related social anxiety disorder, rest assured that you can give a memorable and effective presentation even if you feel nervous—even an elevated level of nervousness. Just imagine how nervous Dr. Martin Luther King, Jr. surely felt standing on the steps of the Lincoln Memorial delivering a televised speech to hundreds of thousands of fellow civil-rights proponents during the March on Washington on August 28, 1963. Yet, he still delivered one of the most important speeches in U.S. history.

> *You can give a memorable and effective presentation even if you feel nervous.*

While experience and practice will help make nervous energy manageable and even productive, it will not eliminate it entirely—and that should not be your goal. Trying to eliminate or "overcome" nervousness associated with presenting may have the opposite effect by intensifying those feelings because you are preoccupied internally with awareness of nervousness instead of externally with connection to audience members.

It is better to expect and accept that you will be nervous. You can then gauge your success on other factors, such as the reaction of audience members, winning a new client or closing a sale, changing audience attitudes toward a subject, teaching listeners a useful skill, strengthening your connection with listeners, engaging listeners in a robust discussion, or receiving positive feedback on evaluation forms or a performance review.

Nervous energy doesn't have to be detrimental, distracting, or even noticeable to listeners. Rather, the goal is for speakers to channel nervous energy into enthusiasm, energy, and dynamism.

Put It in Perspective

Remember, your speech is just a speech. It is not a life-or-death situation, as much your amygdala would lead you to believe. Think through the worst-case scenarios—a prospective client rejects your proposal, a "Zoombomber" displays inappropriate content during an online presentation, you completely forget what you were planning to say, you get a question that you can't answer off the top of your head, or the technology fails in the middle of your talk. While not ideal, worst-case scenarios can be managed.

To put your mind at ease, prepare a contingency plan for dealing with such scenarios ahead of your presentation. For example, practice what you could say to turn a client's rejection into an opportunity to strengthen the relationship and improve your next proposal; plan how you would remove a participant from a virtual meeting; craft an outline that allows you to get back on message if you lose your train of thought; rehearse "thanks-for-your-question-and-I'll-have-to-get-back-to-you-on-that" responses for times when audience members stump you during Q&A; or enlist the help of a co-host or co-producer to help with audience and technology management during technical glitches.

Show Yourself Grace

Also, remember not to be your own worst critic. There is no such thing as a perfect speech. Don't aim for perfection; aim for your best. Presenters often assume that audience members are picking out small flaws like a mispronounced word or a typo on a slide. They aren't—listeners either care for you or just don't care at all.

A more crucial issue than critical audience members is distracted ones. As we all know first-hand from listening to virtual presentations and participating in online meetings, e-mail notifications and the family pet are now competing for audience attention.

Even when you do keep listeners engaged, they most likely will be unaware of hiccups in your speech unless you point them out with disclaimers (like apologizing that your voice is hoarse) or showing signs of frustration (like furrowing your brow or muttering a side comment about a problem with the technology). And if they do notice, they certainly don't judge mistakes as harshly as we judge them ourselves.

Audience members want you to succeed. No one wins if your presentation bombs. Listeners don't want to waste time by sitting through a presentation that stinks; they don't want to waste money by attending a webinar or conference that doesn't contain useful information; and they certainly don't want to feel nervous or embarrassed for a speaker who is struggling. Audiences want a competent, confident, and knowledgeable speaker to guide them through the presentation.

Prepare to Speak Confidently

In addition to setting realistic expectations for nervousness, putting presentations in perspective, and showing yourself grace when things go wrong, you can increase your confidence with long-, mid-, and short-term strategies for success.

In the Long-term, You Can Gain Experience By:

- Taking advantage of opportunities to speak and get feedback—at work, in classes and training programs, and at professional associations and volunteer groups you belong to. Organizations like Toastmasters International, a renowned network of clubs dedicated to helping members become better public speakers and leaders, are excellent resources. Many of these groups formed to practice public speaking now have virtual options. So, they not only provide an excellent way to build confidence without the commute, but they also offer the opportunity to gain experience as a virtual presenter.

- Using everyday encounters to improve your speaking abilities. If you know you tend to speak softly, focus on speaking loudly when you are ordering at a busy restaurant or speaking to an acquaintance while wearing a mask. If you punctuate your speaking with "ums" and "ahs," take care to avoid such words when contributing an opinion in a meeting. You don't have to land a speaking role at a conference or during the quarterly board meeting to gain experience as a presenter.

In the Mid-term, Before an Upcoming Presentation:

- Block adequate time on your calendar for the process of crafting and rehearsing material (at least a month for a major speech and a week for a short or informal presentation).

- Practice at least six times to gain command of the material. (See chapter 17 for more on rehearsals.)

- Record and review your sixth rehearsal to ensure that nervous energy is not detrimental and used productively to convey confidence.

- Do at least one dress rehearsal in the actual speaking space or using the videoconference platform to become comfortable with the technology.

- Consider hiring a coach to streamline the process of crafting material, offer accountability for rehearsals, provide feedback and guidance, and optimize communication outcomes.

In the Short-term, Specifically on the Day of a Presentation:

- Run through your pre-speaking routine. A pre-speaking routine gets you ready to mentally and physically perform at your best on the day of your important presentation. Elite athletes follow a careful routine for eating, hydrating, dressing, focusing, stretching, and warming up on the morning of an important race or match. Similarly, public speakers should not overlook those essential elements that contribute to peak performance, whether they're interviewing for a job, pitching a client, moderating a panel, toasting a friend, or keynoting a conference.

It takes trial and error to identify what helps you speak at your best. Consider the following elements when you develop your pre-speaking routine for the first time.

Fuel

Foods you eat on the day of a presentation should provide energy; they shouldn't slow you down or threaten to upset your stomach. Play with the timing of the last meal or snack you eat before your presentation. Fluid intake is also important. Hydrate in the days leading up to a presentation. Avoid drinking caffeinated beverages right before speaking, as they can make you jittery and also stress the vocal cords. Be aware that very hot and very cold beverages might also affect you negatively. It is better to hydrate with room-temperature water starting at least one day before a presentation. If you chug water right before your presentation, you might find yourself focusing more on a bathroom break than connecting with your audience.

Mental Exercises

No amount of rehearsal will result in an excellent performance if you do not believe in yourself. It is vitally important to focus mentally before a speech. Every speaker develops methods to generate confidence in the hours leading up to a presentation. Yours might include listening to special music, reading inspirational quotations, repeating a mantra, practicing relaxation techniques, visualizing speaking success, or engaging in deep breathing (such as slowly breathing in to the count of four and out to the count of five).

Physical Exercises

In order to perform at your peak, it is important to warm up the muscles of your body and voice beforehand. Consider exercising the morning of your presentation or taking a brisk walk shortly before it is set to begin. Do some stretches like those learned through participation in a sport or activity. Focus especially on loosening up the shoulders, chest, neck, and jaw—all areas where speakers commonly carry tension. If you practice yoga, a series of sun salutations will fit the bill. Remember to warm up your mouth by blowing air through your lips and your jaw by yawning. To warm up your voice, sing in the shower or repeat the following tongue twisters, as well as any of your own favorites, five times in a low, loud, slow, and clear voice:

- Red leather, yellow leather
- Blue leather, black leather
- Dig a big pig
- Sushi chef
- Giggle gaggle
- Unique New York
- Toy boat
- All I want is a proper pot of coffee, made in a proper copper coffee pot

Final Run Through

Run through your entire talk, or the introduction and conclusion of a longer presentation, one final time on the day of your presentation, ideally in the presentation space and using the technology you will use for the actual speech. One of the biggest contributors to nervousness is fear of the unknown. Get comfortable with the format of the program, order of speakers, technology setup, stage setup, and any other variables.

Mark Twain was right when he said that nervousness comes with the territory of public speaking, but it doesn't have to be crippling. You can manage nerves by talking to your doctor about social anxiety disorders (as needed), being realistic in your expectations of nervousness, putting presentations in perspective, showing yourself grace when mistakes happen, and preparing adequately to bolster your confidence.

REMEDIES FOR COMMON SYMPTOMS OF NERVOUSNESS:

Butterflies/upset stomach: Watch what you eat before you present. Eat bland foods, like a banana or a bagel, and stick to room-temperature water. Make sure to have medicine on hand to treat an upset stomach—just in case!

Racing heart/rapid breathing: There is a simple way to help slow a racing heart and rapid breathing—deep breathing. Take a slow, sustained breath in to the count of four and fill your lungs and entire chest cavity with air. Then, in a slow and controlled fashion, exhale to the count of five. Repeat as necessary, slowing the cadence each time to help slow your breathing and heart rate.

Turning red in the face: You can't necessarily prevent your cheeks from turning red, but you can avoid wearing reds and oranges, colors that will highlight the redness. Go with colors on the opposite side of the color wheel that de-emphasize blushing such as greens and blues. Also, wear a shirt with a high neckline.

Quivering voice: Speak loudly. The softer you speak, the more your voice can waver. If you focus on using a commanding voice, you will find that the quiver goes away.

APPLICATION

1. Write down a pre-speaking routine, noting the specific activity you will do and when you will do it. Go through the routine before your next presentation and take note of what you did and when you did it. After the presentation, reflect on the elements of your pre-speaking routine. Was your routine practical? If not, how could you modify it to increase the chances that you will use it in the future? How effective was your routine in lowering your level of nervousness? Are there other elements that you should add? Are there elements that you should refine, adjust the timing of, or eliminate? Edit your pre-speaking routine in preparation for your next presentation accordingly.

2. Fill out the Personal Report of Public Speaking Anxiety (PRPSA; available online) before your next speaking role. Retake it before a similar speaking role in six weeks and again after six months to compare your scores and measure progress.

Notes:

1. "What are Americans Afraid Of?" *The Bruskin Report* (July 1973), 53.

2. Anna Carolina Ferreira Marinho, Adriane Mesquita de Medeiros, Ana Cristina Côrtes Gama, and Letícia Caldas Teixeira, "Fear of Public Speaking: Perception of College Students and Correlates," *Journal of Voice* 31, no. 1 (2017): 127.e7-127.e11.

3. Tomas Furmark, Maria Tillfors, P-O. Everz, Ina Marteinsdottir, Ola Gefvert, and Mats Fredrikson. "Social Phobia in the General Population: Prevalence and Sociodemographic Profile," *Social Psychiatry and Psychiatric Epidemiology* 34, no. 8 (1999): 416-424.

4. Rosemary Black, "Glossophobia (Fear of Public Speaking): Are you Glossophobic?," *Psycom*, accessed May 18, 2022, https://www.psycom.net/glossophobia-fear-of-public-speaking.

5. Glenn Croston, "The Thing We Fear More Than Death," *Psychology Today*, November 29, 2012, https://www.psychologytoday.com/us/blog/the-real-story-risk/201211/the-thing-we-fear-more-death.

Chapter 3

AUDIENCE AND OCCASION

In 1996, Bill Gates published an essay on the Microsoft website titled "Content is King." He wrote, "Content is where I expect much of the real money will be made on the Internet, just as it was in broadcasting."[1] He meant that the success of companies on the Internet will hinge on their ability to provide compelling, high-quality, timely, and relevant material to users. Similarly, the success of presenters hinges on their ability to provide compelling, high-quality, timely, and relevant material to listeners.

To craft content that proves interesting and useful, effective speakers must first take time to analyze their audience and speaking situation. This practice is not new. In ancient Greece, Aristotle categorized types of audiences, speaking situations, and the types of appeals they would find persuasive.

During the pandemic, the analysis of audience and situation went by the wayside for many professionals. It is easy to understand why. For starters, the audience was not in the room. Sometimes they were in little boxes on a videoconference gallery; at other times, they had no visual presence at all because cameras were off. In addition, the situation always seemed the same to speakers: I'm at home wearing sweatpants, slippers, and a more presentable shirt, and talking into a camera on my computer.

It is important to recommit to analyzing the audience and situation—whether you are speaking to no-visible audience members on Zoom, to listeners wearing masks and widely spaced around a conference table, or to an auditorium full of unmasked people who are packed in shoulder-to-shoulder. This analysis provides the foundation for all decisions regarding your presentation, providing a logical place to begin this section of the book on content.

We will turn to our colleague Dr. Jean Miller for a handy tool she learned from her mentor Hester Provensen on how to analyze the key elements of the audience and situation. This process is useful and important whether you are preparing a keynote address or anticipating ways you can contribute to a meeting. These elements are encapsulated in one simple question: *Why am I speaking to this audience on this occasion?*

Here is each step in the five-part *Why Am I* Exercise:

1. Why?

Why am I giving this presentation? Of course, the answer to this question reveals your motivation: What is my purpose? How do I want my listeners to feel, think or behave at the end of my presentation? What is the best-case-scenario outcome?

Take care to assess the feasibility of your goal. Attention spans are short, and many argue they are getting shorter, especially in virtual-communication situations because Zoom fatigue among listeners is real and distractions at home are more numerous. It is a good idea to narrow the scope of what you are informing listeners about and to take smaller steps in the process of persuasion. Trying to push listeners too far, too fast can actually have a "boomerang effect" where listeners move further from your position rather than closer to it.

> *Trying to push listeners too far, too fast can actually have a "boomerang effect" where listeners move further from your position rather than closer to it.*

2. Am I?

Why am I credible on the topic? What unique perspective do I have that my audience can benefit from? What can I offer my audience that no one else can? What relevant information can I provide for someone introducing me to bolster my credibility? What stories can I share or experiences can I mention early in my presentation to position me as an expert on this topic (by way of my educational, professional, and/or personal experience)?

3. Speaking?

Why am I speaking rather than delivering the same content in a written document, pre-recorded video, or other medium? How can I leverage two-way communication in a synchronous format? What interactive discussion, brainstorming, demonstration, activity, and other element can I incorporate to make it a productive use of time? How can I leverage tools on virtual platforms, such as polls, raise of hands, yes and no buttons, chat, whiteboard, break-out rooms, screen sharing to achieve my goals? And also, how can I use only that which is necessary and helpful without inviting a host of glitches and distractions?

4. To This Audience?

Who is in my audience? Where is the intersection between what I know and what they care about? Does this audience have prior experience with the topic or resistance to my perspective? How can I craft my message to resonate most effectively with this particular audience?

Don't make assumptions. Learn what type of listeners you are addressing in terms of their demographics as well as attitudes, beliefs, and values. For meetings and small-group presentations, check LinkedIn profiles of attendees, do some Googling, and ask your colleagues what they know about listeners. For speeches to large audiences, organizations and event planners often have demographic data they can share with you. To get more nuanced information, create your own online survey to send to audience members beforehand and interview a few expected attendees by phone (see the application section at the end of this chapter).

The goal here isn't to alter your speech or insult your audience based on stereotypes of listeners (e.g., making your materials pink when speaking to an audience of women). It also isn't to pander to audience members and tell them what they want to hear; changing your views based on your audience is unethical. Audience analysis is about finding the intersection of what you know, what audience members need to know, and what the occasion calls for. That is the sweet spot where excellent in-person, hybrid, and virtual presentations happen.

> *Audience analysis is about finding the intersection of what you know, what audience members need to know, and what the occasion calls for.*

5. On This Occasion?

On a micro-level, find out all the details you can about the speaking situation: What is the nature of the event at which I am speaking? Are there other presenters or dignitaries in attendance or speaking? What is the history of the event or the context in which it is being held? Will it be in person, partially remote, or fully remote? If in person, what technology will be available to me (microphone, computer, projector, screen, slide advancer, etc.)? If there is a virtual component, what videoconference or webinar platform will be used? What functionality do I have access to on the videoconference platform? How might these factors influence the people and events I recognize during the presentation, the material I use to make my points, and the ways I interact with listeners?

On the meso-level, think about what is going on in the organization or industry. Are attendees transitioning back to fully in-person work this month? Did the organization recently get acquired by a larger company? Is revenue at an all-time high? How might these factors influence the tenor of the event and readiness of listeners to take a course of action?

On the macro-level, consider current events and how they might impact your presentation or audience members. What is the status of the pandemic? What global conflicts are weighing on the minds of listeners? What high-profile crimes or court cases are they following closely? What weather events may be impacting them? What holidays and religious observances are occurring that could impact attendance, attention, and even dietary restrictions?

Asking the question "Why am I speaking to this audience on this occasion?" is a useful activity to work through before every presentation to help ensure that your content is top notch. The answers will provide the information you need to craft material that resonates with listeners, regardless of the occasion, whether they are online, in person, or both.

A QUICK GUIDE TO GENERAL PURPOSES

When asking yourself "Why" in the "Why am I" exercise above, you need not limit yourself to one general purpose of informing or persuading. It is common to have more than one general purpose. Just remember to identify the ratio (e.g., primarily persuasive and secondarily informative, or primarily celebratory and secondarily inspirational) and consider its appropriateness given the speaker, audience, and occasion. Though informing and persuading are the most common presentation purposes in the workplace, the following describe the range of general purposes a speaker might have for a presentation:

To Inform

Informative speaking is aimed at enlightening listeners. It can provide a description, definition, demonstration, update, or combination thereof, and can come in the form of a briefing, report, training program, webinar, lecture, or other educational session. If your goal is for audience members to understand or know something new at the end of your presentation, you are informing. But, if you want listeners to take an action—to approve a budget, select an option, cast a vote, support a plan, donate to a cause, or act on a recommendation—your purpose is primarily persuasive.

If your primary goal truly is to inform, consider ways to make your material relevant, comprehensible, and memorable. Ask yourself: Why should listeners care? How does my subject pertain to their lives or interests? What metaphors, analogies, or other comparisons can I make to help audience members understand this concept? What mnemonic device might I use to help listeners remember main points or steps in an important process? What visuals can I use to show my audience what I mean? How can I narrow my focus to make it more feasible for listeners, especially if my presentation is co-mediated? (See chapter 20 for more on informing.)

To Persuade

Persuasive speaking has the goal of changing the attitudes, beliefs, or actions of audience members. It is the heart of most public speaking courses or training programs, and central to the success of many professionals, whether they are trying to land a job, secure a raise, sell a product or service, pitch an idea, win an argument, or change a policy.

If you are preparing a persuasive presentation, it is important to ask: How will audience members benefit personally by accepting the position? Where do listeners stand on the issue and how far can I reasonably change their position in the time and format I have available for my speech? What can I do to bolster my credibility? How can I make listeners care about my topic? How do I make the strongest case for my argument? (See chapter 22 for more on persuading.)

To Celebrate

Celebratory speeches often occur at important rites of passage in life—like a milestone birthday, graduation, wedding, anniversary, retirement, and even death. These special occasion speeches are important opportunities to let the important people in our lives know how much they mean to us.

When crafting a speech with a primary purpose of celebrating a person or honoring their accomplishments, ask yourself: How can I succinctly explain my connection to the subject? What characteristics of the person are worthy of praise and what anecdotes highlight those traits? Who else needs to be thanked or acknowledged for helping this person reach their achievements? How can I situate this person's accomplishments into a larger context or give them greater meaning to the community of listeners?

To Inspire

Managers, executives, politicians, preachers, military authorities, and other leaders may find themselves in a position to deliver an inspirational or motivational message at moments of crisis. Sir Winston Churchill, the prime minister of the United Kingdom during some of the darkest days of World War II, immediately comes to mind (his 1940 "Blood, Toil, Tears and Sweat," is an excellent place to start if you are unfamiliar with famous oratory). Inspirational speaking is also seen among headliners at industry conferences, self-improvement seminars, and school assemblies.

If the focus of your presentation is to motivate or inspire, consider asking yourself: How do I want audience members to approach life differently when they leave my presentation? What personal experiences and inspiring stories of others can I draw upon to connect with listeners? How can I reveal a personal fault or flaw in my story that will provide a poignant lesson to my audience?

To Entertain

Entertainment is often a secondary or tertiary purpose of presentations—think of a humorous how-to speech or Mindy Kaling's 2018 commencement address at Dartmouth College. Though it is less common for the primary speech purpose to be entertainment, you can find this focus in after-dinner speeches, such as those given by the president and others at the White House Correspondents' Dinner, as well as roasts. Keep in mind, a speech aimed to entertain is not the same as stand-up comedy. The former is a speech with an introduction, body, and conclusion; the latter is a series of one-liners. Also, audiences bristle at mean-spirited jokes (e.g., Chris Rock at the 2022 Academy Awards). The most effective type of humor is self-deprecating.

When preparing a speech to entertain, ponder these questions: What is my underlying theme or message? Who will get the humor (is it only for a few insiders)? How can I make jokes at my own expense? Would my grandparent be offended by the humor or language? How can I make the humor relevant to the listeners and what they care about?

At first glance, informative and persuasive speech purposes seem most relevant for workplace presentations. But, as you manage teams, direct departments, run organizations, or become a thought leader in an industry, you will find that celebrating, inspiring, and entertaining are vital speech purposes to utilize as well.

APPLICATION

1. Dig deeper into your audience analysis. Conduct 15-minute phone interviews with several audience members (event organizers are pleased to provide contact information). During your conversations, find out what each person does, where they are from, why they are attending the event at which you will be speaking, concerns they have about your topic, and what they hope to learn from your presentation. Don't keep to a strict list of questions. Have some open-ended questions prepared to keep the conversation flowing but listen carefully and follow the lead of the person you're interviewing.

2. Customize your presentation and make it resonate with your listeners by collecting several interesting stories and examples from your conversations and incorporating them into your presentation. Make sure to ask permission before using any specific information.

Notes:

1. Bill Gates, "Content is King," *Microsoft.com*, January 6, 1996, accessed June 21, 2022, http://www.microsoft.com/billgates/columns/1996essay/essay960103.asp.
Archived at https://bit.ly/3c2EJ7Q

Chapter 4

TOPIC AND THESIS

Topic selection might seem self-evident. For many presentations, the topic appears obvious because it has been assigned to you or it is a normal occurrence in your profession.

Indeed, all presentations involve choices. Most of us recognize this in presentations that are more open-ended or personal. For example, TED-style presentations clearly involve choices because speakers are not being assigned topics, nor are these types of presentations routine even for folks who have given many of them. Still, presentations where you might believe your job is simply to relay the facts also involve choices in what is said and left unsaid, the order of importance, and even word selection.

Presentations are more effective when we make *active choices* to select a topic, move toward a general purpose, and construct a thesis. The benefit of this perspective is a shift in mindset. When a presenter approaches topic selection as a passive assignment, it can feel boring, formulaic, or hackneyed. None of these feelings are inspiring as a presenter, and they certainly are not likely to translate into a successful presentation to your audience.

> *Presentations are more effective when we make active choices to select a topic, move toward a general purpose, and construct a thesis.*

Shifting to an active choice mindset in topic selection invites more critical thinking, which in turn can make the presentation more meaningful to you and your audience. The following are considerations for this process.

The Speaker

In chapter 3 on audience and occasion, we breakdown the component parts of the guiding question: "Why am I speaking to this audience on this occasion?" For topic selection, the "I" matters more than we often account for. Many presentations in which topics are passively received have a strong sense of routine, tradition, or duty, which de-emphasizes the individual speaker. The presenter can feel like a conduit of information, merely a vessel providing a message, an interchangeable part to deliver the content. Filtering topic selection through your own experience and expertise can shift the focus onto information that you are uniquely suited to deliver. It can turn a mundane presentation into something that you are excited to deliver. Or, if you have been given tremendous freedom in topic selection for a presentation, focusing on your own expertise, experience, and excitement can decrease the stress of picking a topic.

For presenters who are invited to speak at a conference or other event, you will be well-served by allowing your personal interests and experiences to guide your decision to accept or decline the invitation. After all, if you accept an invitation to speak on a subject you lack knowledge of or care about, you will frustrate yourself and disappoint your listeners.

It is always flattering to receive an invitation to present, but resist the temptation to give an immediate "yes." Ask the event organizer about the desired topic of your talk. Only accept if you can speak with enthusiasm and credibility on a topic that is appropriate for the situation and audience, and if you have the bandwidth to prepare properly.

When the desired speech topic doesn't speak to your passions, interests, or expertise, suggest related topics that do. If you are unable to find a topic that works for both you and the event organizer, politely decline. You need not worry about upsetting the person who invited you. It would be far worse to accept and do a disservice to the audience and event than it would be to decline. To soften the blow of declining, you might suggest other speakers you know and respect who could do justice to the topic.

Sometimes it might feel like you have very little agency in making an active choice. There are other factors demanding that you give a presentation that you must give, but you did not actively choose the topic and simply cannot see yourself in it. We hope these moments are very few, but in those moments, focus on excellence. Deliver the best version of the required presentation.

Audience

Starting topic selection with the speaker helps to build confidence. Nevertheless, it cannot stop there. We speak to be heard, and that means actively choosing topics to consider your audience. Note that audience adaptation is not the same as pandering. The former has to do with framing your message in a way that will resonate with listeners; the latter has to do with changing your message to appeal to a particular audience. Pandering is neither advisable nor ethical (see chapter 1 for details on ethics).

Tailoring your message to your audience requires thinking about how to share your passion, experience, or expertise in a way that will be valuable. It is the process of translating what you know to other people.

For example, imagine you work in grassroots advocacy in North Dakota. You are an expert in wildlife preservation on the Great Plains. Speaking to an audience of North Dakotans might be different from speaking at a national conference. You certainly could pre-package a presentation to both audiences, but a better choice would be to select a more locally known topic for the residents of the state and opt for something with national resonance for the conference. Both can connect with your expertise and both can excite you. And, because you tried to account for—but not pander to—your audience, you can deliver a presentation that sticks with your listeners.

Considering the audience and yourself as you define the topic begins the process of building a relationship between speaker and listener. If you have that in mind from the beginning, crafting and conveying the presentation is far more likely to build a strong relationship.

Considering the audience and yourself as you define the topic begins the process of building a relationship between speaker and listener.

The Situation

Lastly, don't overlook the situational demands that can impact topic selection. Expectations are part of the situation. Ceremonial speeches, like a commencement address or wedding toast, have certain generic expectations that have developed through repetition and time. The same is true for other forms of speaking. In some academic disciplines, it is the norm to read a manuscript presentation. In other disciplines, the standard is to speak more extemporaneously. Expectations might even be specific to your firm, company, or organization. There might just be "The Acme Way" with regards to presentations. At the level of topic selection, of course you want to be aware of these expectations, but if there is "The Acme Way" and possibly a better way, then make an active choice about it.

For example, when you are presenting as part of a continuing education or mandatory training program, be aware that your listeners might be reluctant to participate. Granted, they signed up for the class and ostensibly have a desire to learn, but, in many cases, learners are required to take and attend classes. As such, the bar for engaging listeners is higher than if audience members had sought out an opportunity to hear you speak. If the expectation is a boring, data-dump of a presentation, does it need to be that way? Can you shift from a topic of "Everything you need to know about X" to "What you need to know about X right now"? If you feel dissatisfied with how such presentations are received when you align with the expected topics and modes, or if your audience is not receptive to the expected topics and modes, then it seems there is an opportunity to make a different choice.

Another part of the situation is the moment, which implies the immediate context and timeliness. When new information emerges that you think is interesting, that you have experience about, and that you deem is relevant to your audience, you might need to shift your topic to account for this timely event.

There are also occasions that call for a public address where you have been selected to speak—commencement addresses and award-acceptance speeches are a few examples. Your topic must be authentic to your interests, responsive to the needs of the audience, and sensitive to the demands of the situation.

At the end of this chapter, we have listed numerous general purposes and some key questions that you might ask yourself to determine if that purpose fits the presentation you are giving. Most presentations are a hybrid of multiple purposes, but there is likely a primary purpose that you feel is most important.

Thesis

Don't confuse purpose with your message, which is what you are trying to say in your speech. The message is your thesis, and can also be called the specific purpose, central idea, or controlling idea. Your thesis should be a simple and singular sentence whether you are speaking in person or in technology-mediated contexts.

The thesis should state a position—even if it is a routine project update or summary of research conducted. You should be able to put the words "I believe" in front of your thesis statement and have it make sense. For example, it wouldn't make sense to say, "I believe project update" or "I believe research conducted." Instead, your thesis might be "I believe the project is on track for completion in Q3" or "I believe the Acme case precedent will best support our client's legal claim." You don't have to actually say the "I believe" in your presentation—we know you believe it because you are saying it—but the practice of testing your thesis with "I believe" will help you transition from a general topic to a specific thesis statement that makes a claim based on your knowledge, expertise, and perspective. It will help you, the speaker, make an active choice regarding the perspective you want to share with listeners.

Simplicity

The ideas contained within a presentation do not need to be simple, but your expression of these ideas does. Unlike the written word, listeners can't easily revisit a thesis statement that they don't understand.

Once a presentation is delivered, it usually disappears into the ether. If audience members are confused or unable to remember a key point, they don't have the luxury of rewinding the presentation. Although presentations can be recorded, do you really want to rely on listeners to rewatch it in order to understand it? Chances are they won't go back. And ironically, the speeches that audiences will seek out to watch again are simple, straightforward ones that they connected with, remembered, and liked the most.

How do you achieve simplicity in your thesis statement? Keep it short and direct; avoid using a comma, "and," or other grammatical tools to connect ideas, and distill your message to its most basic form.

GOOD, BETTER, BEST

Here are a few good, better, and best theses from informative and persuasive presentations:

Informative briefing

- Good: The new workflow management system.
- Better: The developments in the new workflow management system impact all employees, including managers and associates.
- Best: Updates to the workflow management system impact all employees.

Persuasive pitch

- Good: Let me tell you why you need Acme widgets.
- Better: In order to help you solve your current problems with connectivity, Acme widgets provide options for offices of all kinds.
- Best: Acme widgets are the best solution to connectivity problems in hybrid workplaces.

Singularity

Your presentation should have laser focus. The topic must be narrow and specific, and even more so in virtual presentations when attention easily wanes and time limits are truncated. It is important to recognize that singularity should not be mistaken for obscurity. The purpose of being focused is to better connect with the audience, not to drive them away. Your objective is to tell listeners something they don't know, have them understand it, and get them to remember it. To do this you must drill down on a topic. Go for depth, not breadth.

One last word of advice, don't combine your thesis and preview. Unlike what you might have been taught in writing classes, separating the thesis and the preview of your key points is a good idea when giving a presentation. You want to present your most important information in digestible and memorable pieces. A main idea combined with a multi-clause preview of the key points in a speech is less likely to stick in the minds of the audience. Separate the two. (See chapter 9 for more on signposting and a checklist for speech introductions on page 84.)

APPLICATION

1. Identify a presentation you have on your calendar or an update you must give in an upcoming meeting. Imagine that the event or meeting is running behind and you have to deliver your message in an abbreviated fashion. Give the one-minute version of your presentation. Then, give the 30-second version. Finally, distill it to one sentence that makes sense when you start it with "I believe." If you do not overtly say this one sentence in the full-length version of your presentation (sans "I believe"), incorporate it (ideally after your attention getter and before your preview of main points).

2. Write your thesis in a number of different ways. Brainstorm in a way that doesn't feel permanent, such as on a piece of scratch paper, a notes app, or a new Word document. Try to use different words each time. After you have 3–5 options, identify what words, phrasings, or approaches resonate with you. As you mix and match, transfer the best options to your presentation outline and create your best version of the thesis.

Chapter 5

THE SANDWICH STRUCTURE

From university students we have taught to senior executives we have coached, speakers of all experience levels want to give the best possible presentation with the smallest investment of time. However, many are not equipped with tools to achieve that goal.

Some presenters script their remarks word for word and read them or try to commit them to memory. This approach is extremely time consuming and often leads to the wooden delivery of content better suited to the printed page. The pandemic has caused a rise in scripting and reading because online presenters mistakenly believe listeners can't tell. Sorry to burst your bubble, but they see your eyes moving side to side as you read off the page instead of looking into the camera lens, and they hear that you sound scripted and not conversational.

> *The pandemic has caused a rise in scripting and reading because online presenters mistakenly believe listeners can't tell.*

Other speakers struggle to get started. They have ideas but get overwhelmed looking at a blank sheet of paper or an empty set of presentation slides on their computer screen. As a result, they waste time and end up with a hastily prepared and under-rehearsed speech, or recycled remarks that do not fit the speaking occasion.

These common speech-crafting problems lead to the same result—presentations that are a disappointment to both the audience and speaker. It doesn't have to be that way.

We have developed a method of outlining presentations called the Sandwich Structure that can achieve a compelling TED-like presentation style in a reasonable amount of time. Our outline method allows speakers to visualize their whole presentation on one piece of paper as they build it, and later helps them transition from one idea to the next without relying on a script or getting tripped up on exact wording.

This is a unique approach that you won't find in other sources. Speakers swear by it because it is useful for crafting almost any type of presentation and it is particularly conducive to the extemporaneous mode of speaking that we recommend for most workplace situations. As opposed to scripting and reading, scripting and memorizing, or speaking off the cuff, extemporaneous speaking requires careful research that is translated into a detailed and logical outline that the presenter rehearses thoroughly and delivers dynamically. Our Sandwich Structure method offers a straightforward and reliable process that is useful for a wide range of speaking roles, as well as a step-by-step procedure that prevents writer's block. Additionally, it encourages clear and memorable content, incorporates best practices of public speaking, and just as importantly, saves valuable time.

> *This is a unique approach that you won't find in other sources.*

Here Is How It Works:

The Sandwich Structure rejects word for word scripts that often lead to a stiff and inauthentic delivery style. Instead, it embraces and adapts the Roman Numeral Outline you may have learned at some point in your schooling to organize papers. It adapts the Roman Numeral Outline in four important aspects to meet the demands and acknowledge the best practices of public speaking. Following are the four ways the Sandwich Structure differs from a Roman Numeral Outline:

1. It limits the outline to one page.

2. It is oriented horizontally rather than vertically.

3. It is stacked like a "Sandwich," with a section at the top and at the bottom for the speech attention getter and clincher.

4. It includes visual cues to remind speakers to incorporate several best practices of public speaking.

One Page

The first way the Sandwich Structure differs from a Roman Numeral Outline is that it is always on one sheet of paper. It doesn't matter if it's a two-minute report or two-hour webinar. By limiting notes to just one page, the Sandwich Structure prevents a scripted presentation because speakers must limit their outline to key words and phrases. This saves vast amounts of preparation time and improves speech delivery because it promotes extemporaneous speaking encouraging speakers to take brief glances at their well-rehearsed notes, make eye contact with their audience, and then talk to listeners about each idea using a conversational tone.

Oriented Horizontally

Next, the Sandwich Structure differs from a Roman Numeral Outline because the page orientation is horizontal rather than vertical—organizing the main points on the paper like a timeline from left to right. (See chapter 6 for more on main points.) This orientation is crucial for extemporaneous speaking because it allows speakers to find their next idea quickly. When you are moving from one point to the next, or worse, at those moments in a presentation when you completely lose your train of thought and freeze, the Sandwich Structure helps you recover quickly because you have the security of knowing exactly where to look on the outline to find your next point.

With the outline limited to one page and oriented horizontally, you always know that notes related to the beginning of your speech are on the left-hand side of the paper. In the middle of the presentation, the notes are right in the middle of the page. And toward the end of your speech, you need only to glance to the right-hand side of the paper to find the word or phrase you wrote down to jog your memory for that part of your presentation.

Speaking from a Sandwich Structure Outline and in the extemporaneous mode is uncomfortable for some speakers at first, as is doing anything new. However, with a little practice, you will find it easy to glance down at your one-page outline in the correct part of the page, find the word or phrase for the next idea in your speech, look up at the audience, smile, and speak with confidence.

The horizontal orientation also can be a tremendous time saver because it allows speakers to diagnose problems with their speech content early in the outlining process. If in an early iteration of the Sandwich Structure you notice that the first point in your speech has six sub-points, but the second has only two, it is immediately clear the presentation lacks balance. This knowledge suggests that the organization should be reconsidered; perhaps the first main point should become the subject of the entire speech, or maybe the first main point could be broken into two smaller and more manageable main points.

If you write out an entire script for a speech, chances are you will have spent much more time on the content before you realize there are issues with the supporting material or organization. Worse yet, you may never develop a clear thesis or carefully structured main points to support it—obstacles the Sandwich Structure prompts you to resolve concisely and early in the process of crafting presentation content.

The Sandwich

The third difference between the Sandwich Structure and a Roman Numeral Outline is the presence of a "Sandwich," the namesake of this method of outlining, which refers to the portion of the page at the top and bottom of the outline that is sectioned off from the speech body with horizontal lines. The top and bottom of the Sandwich are sectioned off so you can write the first line or two and the last line or two of the speech. Why, you might ask, would the opening and closing of the presentation be written out after great pains were taken to describe the Sandwich Structure as a rejection of a scripted approach?

Because the introduction and conclusion are the most important parts of a presentation. According to the basic psychological principles of primacy and recency, people most vividly remember what they hear first and last. This holds true for presentations as well, so you must make your opening and closing count. (See chapter 7 for more on introducing and concluding.)

Don't waste the opening lines of your speech providing biographical information about yourself (that is the purpose of having someone else give the speaker introduction), repeating the title or main idea of your presentation (you will get to this after the opening lines), or thanking the person who introduced you or the event organizer (you can thank the introducer as you acknowledge the host after your attention getter and before you get into the body of your speech). The first words out of your mouth must be interesting, catchy, and suspenseful. You want those words to grab the attention of audience members and give them a reason to continue listening. (See chapter 7 for detail on crafting attention getters.)

The concluding lines of your presentation are equally important. They must signal the presentation is coming to a close so listeners know you have finished and they can clap, ask questions, or move on to the next presenter (whatever is appropriate to the situation). A strong conclusion will prevent an awkward silence after your last line and means you will never have to say an uninspiring "thank-you" or "that's it" as the last words of your presentation. Accomplish this by coming full circle—your clincher should refer, in some concrete way, to your attention getter. Effective closings also offer listeners pause for thought or an actual call to action to challenge them to change their beliefs or actions. (See chapter 7 for detail on crafting clinchers.)

The Sandwich element of the Sandwich Structure ensures a robust, well-planned introduction and conclusion because these sections are written out in advance and, ideally, memorized. If nerves cause you to blank out on the introduction or conclusion during a presentation, the lines are in front of you for last-minute review, and in worst-case scenarios, available for you to read to the audience word-for-word.

Having the Sandwich is crucial to effective speech delivery because having a carefully crafted introduction and conclusion, as well as the security of knowing the lines are there to read if necessary, makes speakers feel more confident. It allows speakers to approach and leave the lectern on a high note, even if there were a few stumbles during the body of the speech.

Ocular Cues

The last way the Sandwich Structure departs from the Roman Numeral Outline is the inclusion of ocular, or visual, reminders to include best practices of public speaking in your presentation.

One best practice that the Sandwich Structure facilitates is overtly stating the central idea. There is a place below the introduction for a speaker to write a word or phrase for the central idea of the speech. Though it sounds obvious, many speakers fail to identify and clearly state the point of their speech early in the presentation (or ever). In most cases, this is advisable and will improve clarity of the overall message. (If you happen to be giving a persuasive speech to an antagonistic audience, however, you would be wise to establish your credibility and provide some support for your case before revealing your specific ask.)

> *Many speakers fail to identify and clearly state the point of their speech early on in the presentation (or ever).*

Additionally, the Sandwich Structure has the word "preview" on the page just below the central idea to remind the speaker to tell audience members at the beginning of the speech how it is structured. This roadmap of the presentation lets listeners know what to expect and promotes the retention of key ideas. Continuing with the sage advice of "tell 'em what you're gonna tell 'em, tell 'em, tell 'em what you told 'em," the Sandwich Structure includes the word "review" just above the conclusion so the speaker is reminded to recap for the audience where they went on the journey of the presentation, as well as to reinforce the main points. (See chapter 8 for more on previews and reviews.)

Finally, the T's with circles around them signal the speaker to transition from one idea in a presentation to the next. This ensures that listeners are never left behind when a speaker moves on to a new main point. It also serves as another way for speakers to emphasize ideas they want audience members to remember. (See chapter 8 for more on transitions.)

Having ocular cues—the central idea, preview, review, and transitions—on the Sandwich Structure reminds speakers to be clear and repetitious, attributes that are particularly crucial when a message is delivered orally rather than in writing, and virtually rather than in person. By using ocular cues, speakers are prompted to follow these best practices of public speaking without a lot of extra text that could hinder locating key ideas and supporting points on the Sandwich Structure while delivering an extemporaneous presentation.

Remember to write your Sandwich Structure in large text on a full sheet of paper that is oriented horizontally. You also can access our online speech-planning tool at https://bit.ly/

SpeechOutlineTool to craft your Sandwich Structure. It provides an easy template to fill in and offers helpful reminders to keep you on track. Using large, legible font (whether hand-written or computer generated) is key to easily read your notes when you refer to them, and readily find the next point on your Sandwich Structure when you "freeze" and can't remember what to say next. The Sandwich Structure provides many speakers peace of mind by knowing exactly where to look to find their next item to present.

Like anything new, the Sandwich Structure will take a little getting used to. With practice, it will save time on crafting a presentation, improve message effectiveness, support an extemporaneous delivery, and even provide the foundation for a TED-style speech with no notes. Soon you will feel more confident and enjoy more success in speaking situations—whether you are an early career professional contributing to meetings or a seasoned leader delivering a keynote address on a stage.

APPLICATION

1. Craft a Sandwich Structure of an upcoming presentation. This might be something as formal as a conference speech or a webinar for prospective clients, or as informal as an update on a project that you will give at a team meeting or an answer to a question you expect to get asked on a scheduled phone call.

2. Look back at an old presentation and ask, "how would I adapt this into the sandwich structure?" You will find that the structure becomes more strategic, the signposting of key ideas becomes crisp, and the beginning and end are more purposeful.

3. Outline a presentation you hear. The value of the Sandwich Structure can become clearer when listening to a presentation and trying to understand its structure and main ideas. If you are on a call as an audience member, outline one of the presentations. Attempt to outline the presentation using the Sandwich Structure, or try to create the conventional Roman Numeral outline. If the speaker made this easy for you, identify the features of the presentation that made outlining easy. If the speaker made the process of outlining difficult for you, what was missing and how did it impact the presentation?

I brought along a few friends to help me tell my story. These are my backyard chickens [sharing image on slide of chickens with names written]. You're probably asking yourself, "Why is Ann up there talking about her chickens?" It turns out, it's a real challenge to count all my chicken and eggs. I need to do that in order to know how much feed to buy and how many eggs I can have for Sunday breakfast. This is actually a really good analogy for the Census and the challenges of counting every single Texan in our beautiful, vast, and rapidly growing state

Everything is bigger in Texas—The impact, the problems, and the heart of those solving them.

T I. Why the Census Matters in Texas...and why Texas matters nationally

PREVIEW

A. Our Voices
- 28M people in Texas, 1 in 11 Americans
- Up to 3 new congressional seats

B. Our Businesses
- Where to set up shop and create new jobs

C. Our Quality of Life
- Fed programs
- 1% undercount = $300M a year
- 8% undercount = 2.4B a year
- Texas is a low-spending state, so fed dollars are even more critical

D. Why Texas matters nationally
- Size of economy
- Outsized influence on politics and policy
- Leading edge of nat'l demographic shift

T II. How the Census Count is at Risk

PREVIEW

A. Texas is big - really big!
- Really 5 states in one—map
- A few factoids about size of Texas
- One of 4 states where POC are a majority

B. Hard-to-Count Communities
- 25% of Texans live in HTC communities—map
- Very young children, immigrants people who live in rural areas

C. Unique challenges
- Lack of funding
- Online forms
- Fear
- Lack of state response

D. Why the lackluster response from the state?
- Citizenship question
- Growth primarily in districts that lean D, R's in power not interested in electing more D's
- Don't believe in govt or fair representation anyway
- Would rather cut off their nose to spite their face

T III. What We Are Doing About It

A. Texas Counts
- We didn't stand idly by
- Campaign and Pooled Fund

B. Campaign
- Mobilizes leaders across the state and sectors
- Steering Committee and subcommittees
- Faith, CBO, education, business, government, health care, philanthropy

REVIEW

The moral of this story is not, "Count your chickens before they hatch." It is, "Count every chicken. Every single one of them." Because the future of our democracy and our communities depends on it. **Watch the speaker's presentation at bit.ly/SampleSandwichStructure**

In our last fiscal year, attorneys and staff at our firm participated in 1070 coaching sessions across all US and UK offices, and across all attorney levels of seniority – summer associates to partners. Coaching is a powerful professional development tool available to you all to help you to be as effective as possible in your roles. Specifically, coaching can help you clarify goals, navigate obstacles, and achieve results.

For those who don't know me, I'm a trained executive coach, and have a long history with the firm. I was an associate here early in my career before moving into a professional development role. I have served as an external executive coach to lawyers at various firms, including ours. I recently rejoined the firm to develop internal training programs including this coaching initiative.

THESIS: *Coaching can help you clarify goals, navigate obstacles, and achieve results:*

PREVIEW

Point 1 – Mia: I'm new to the team and I feel disconnected	Point 2 – Elsa: I'm stressed and don't know how to manage my team	Point 3 – Jack: Should I stay or should I go?
A. Clarified goals · Build strong relationships · Explore the work of various teams B. Navigated obstacles / solutions · Felt unsure about how to forge relationships in a remote environment · Identified the relationships to foster and how · Increased confidence around communicating interests in various practice areas · Developed strategies to influence the type of work she was on C. Results · Improved relationships and was able to increase the amount of work she is doing in areas of interest	A. Clarified goals: · Effectively manage team when workload is heavy B. Navigated obstacles / solutions · Used coaching to gather upward feedback and create and action plan · Developed a roadmap to communicate effectively, manage stress, delegate, give feedback, get feedback, support team, and build trust with team C. Results · Showed an improved ability to prioritize tasks and communicate them to her team, especially when a deadline is looming D. Improved work product from team and for client	A. Clarified goals · Identify next career steps B. Navigated obstacles / solutions · Felt stuck and was unclear of his professional path · Developed a strategy to identify what his path might look like at the firm, what opportunities might exist, and what questions to as a potential in-house employer C. Results · He received an offer from the in-house position, used coaching to work through the decision-making process, and ultimately decided to remain at the firm.

Q&A and REVIEW

1070 hours of coaching this year alone! Now that you know about this voluntary and confidential professional development opportunity, I hope you will be a part of our coaching hour totals and success stories during our next fiscal year, or whenever you are ready for support. If you would like to apply for coaching now or in the future, the next steps are to review our coaching overview, connect with me, and schedule your first coaching session.

Chapter 6

MAIN IDEAS AND THE NARRATIVE ARC

You have been asked to give a brief report on a project. You have been working on this project for a year. You tell yourself, "I know this better than anyone. I'll just hop on the call and we will have a conversation about it." When you start speaking you repeat yourself, you return to previous points to fill in details you left out, you remember an important point that probably should have come first, and at the end of the call, you realize that the information was correct but this conversation was not as productive as you hoped. In what should have been a moment to share your expertise, you worry that the presentation did not convey your preparation or knowledge. Even worse, you fear it undermined your credibility because it lacked focus and a narrative arc.

Constructing main points, even when you are confident about the material, is important both for you and your listeners. If your material is clear, well-explained, logically structured, and confidently delivered, it will help you stay on track and allow your listeners to follow you. Constructing main points plays a major role in accomplishing these ends.

> *Constructing main points, even when you are confident about the material, is important both for you and your listeners.*

How Do I Create Main Points?

If you are not quite sure what to say to support your thesis, compile all the key ideas you might want to convey in one list or on a whiteboard. Use scrap paper or another tool that feels temporary so you are comfortable brainstorming and editing. Once you have recorded all of your ideas, you will notice that some ideas can be combined, some ideas that seemed important don't really fit with the others, some ideas seem to relate to others in specific ways, and other ideas seem less relevant.

After you have brainstormed, review your points and ask yourself if there are any points that need to be added or deleted. In making these decisions, consider how the points relate to:

- Your general purpose, topic, and thesis statement

- The substance of the point

- The composition of the audience

- The expectations of the occasion

For example, you might decide that because of the advanced knowledge base of your audience, a point regarding the background of your project would be unnecessary. Or you might decide that because your purpose is to report on quarterly performance, suggestions for future actions might be a subject for a different time. If you feel a point should still be addressed, perhaps a brief mention in the conclusion rather than a main point would suffice.

At this juncture, you might find it helpful to assign a tentative order to your ideas by numbering them or moving them on the scrap paper, whiteboard, or within the document that you are typing. This process leads to the topic of ordering main points.

How Should I Order My Main Points?

You may have a tentative order in mind, but it might be helpful to think about a few patterns of arrangement that could suit your presentation. There should be a reason why your points occur in the order that they do. This purposeful structure or narrative arc will make it easier for you to remember your main points, for listeners to follow them, and for you to achieve the purpose of your presentation.

> *There should be a reason why your points appear in the order that they do.*

A general reason in selecting a pattern of arrangement is to consider whether your points are logically independent or dependent. Logically independent ideas do not rely upon each other. Each individual point supports the central idea of the presentation. If one point is weak, it has minimal impact on the other main points. On the other hand, logically dependent ideas build upon one another in a chain-like fashion. You need each link in the chain to be strong or the logic of the presentation will break.

Following are several go-to patterns of presentation arrangements ranging from the most casual answer to a question in a routine meeting delivered over the phone to a lengthy and formal address on a stage.

Topical

Also called categorical, this pattern of arrangement selects independent categories that are related to a theme, but not necessarily links in a chain. If you are reporting on the sales performance of two branches of a business, your main points might be online and in-store. Although there will probably be a reason why you place these topics in a specific order, logically you could place them in any order and still meet the purpose of your presentation. In his June 2005 commencement address at Stanford University, Steve Jobs opened with a joke and then previewed the body of his speech by saying, "Today I want to tell you three stories from my life. That's it. No big deal. Just three stories."[1] This powerful topical structure of main ideas encourages storytelling. We call it, "Three Story Structure."

Speakers can use this pattern of arrangement in a wide range of situations—and not just for celebratory speeches or when sharing personal stories. They could share three success stories, case studies, client examples, testimonials, relevant legal precedents, etc. Whatever you call them, structuring main points this way prompts the speaker to share concrete narratives, a practice that for most is more natural, engaging, and memorable than reciting information on three disparate topics. As long as at least one story resonates with listeners, the presentation is effective because each point is logically independent.

Chronological

The benefit to organizing a presentation based on time is its linearity. Time is very orderly, a concept that helps an audience understand the connection between points. Most people think of chronological order as past, present, and future, but a chronological arrangement can also use eras or other time-sequenced events as its markers of time.

Additionally, there might be a reason to change the order. Perhaps you are speaking about the impact of a recent policy on your business's profit. You might begin with the present to note how profits have risen, and then return to the past to show how they got to that point before addressing what action needs to be taken in the future to ensure that profits continue to rise.

If you are using chronological order to set markers of time, your points are logically independent. But when you move into past, present, and future (or some variation thereof) for a persuasive speech, you likely have logically dependent points—meaning that if listeners do not accept earlier points, they will not accept later points.

Spatial

Spatial organization arranges main points in a presentation based on geography, location, or distance. For example, a presentation that discusses changing market forces impacting your business might move from macro to micro beginning with global market forces, then move to U.S. market forces, and then arrive at local market forces. To audience members living in that local area, you have taken them from distant, yet important factors, while gradually covering topics that are closer to their daily lives. Conversely, you could discuss a topic spatially from micro to macro—a closeup to a wide view. This option could help listeners understand the importance of their personal actions (such as avoiding single-use plastic on the environmental health of a region, a nation, and even the world). Spatial organization may be used by an office administrator to talk about how an initiative will be rolled out to offices located in different cities, or by a scientist to explain how a new therapy affects different organs in the body.

Similar to chronological structure, if you are using geographic markers to separate topics, your points are logically independent—each "stop" on your speech journey can stand on its own. But if you move to micro, meso, macro (or the reverse), you likely have logically dependent points that require the acceptance of earlier points to achieve agreement with later points.

Problem-Solution

In problem-solution reasoning, order matters. We don't take action to solve non-existent problems—there are too many other issues that require our attention and resources. In general, if a presenter has done a poor job demonstrating the significance of a problem, an audience is not likely to endorse a plan or feel a sense of urgency to act, no matter how simple or feasible the proposed solution is. This is an example of speech points that are logically dependent.

Causal

Like problem-solution, a cause-and-effect structure requires a close connection between points to yield the greatest impact. For example, what causes the greatest growth in the U.S. economy? Is it reducing taxes? Is it increased taxation with increased government subsidization and reinvestment? Is it a reduction in export regulations? To prove that any one of these is the cause of an improving economy (i.e., the effect), the reasoning must be compelling.

Process of Elimination

The process of elimination is one of the more undervalued patterns of arrangement. This form of reasoning presents a series of points and eliminates each point before moving to the next one, eventually arriving at the last point, which will be the best option. The benefit of this pattern of reasoning is that it allows the audience to understand how the eventual best option was decided. The speaker, like a diligent math student, is showing their work. When audience members feel like they are arriving at a conclusion alongside you, their confidence in the decision will be stronger. Because listeners must accept the arguments you dismiss before arriving at the best option, points structured in this arrangement should be considered logically dependent.

COMMON PATTERNS OF ARRANGEMENT

Informative structures:

- Chronological (past, present, future)
- Spatial (local, state, national; macro, meso, micro)
- Topical (category A, category B, category C)

- Causal (cause-effect)

Persuasive structures:
- Problem-solution

- Spatial (me, us, society)

- Three Story Structure (success story 1, success story 2, success story 3)

- Process of elimination (See more on informative speaking in chapter 20 and persuasive speaking in chapter 22.)

Now What?

The last step in constructing main points is to run a few tests.

Subordination and Balance

First, look at the main points (ideally on your Sandwich Structure Outline from chapter 5) and ask if they are equally important? Is each main point worthy of being a main point and not better suited as support for another main point? If a main point seems to fit within another main point, this subordination means that it was not worthy of main point status. Another part of judging whether points are equally important is balance. Main points should have roughly the same amount of content. If one main point takes five minutes to explain, and the other two main points take two minutes each, the speech will feel top heavy and later points will seem like afterthoughts.

Coordination and Division

Second, ask yourself if the main points act as team players? Like being a member of a team, each main point should coordinate with other points to achieve a common goal. And, as part of a team, the main points should each contribute something unique to the effort. If two main points do the same thing, they are not contributing as separate ideas towards the purpose of the presentation.

Some of the most common problems with coordination and division occur because we rely on default settings in our speaking and fail to ask if those settings fit the current speaking situation. To continue the team metaphor, the strategy that worked ten years, a year, or even a week ago might not work in the situation that you face today.

Problems with coordination and division are more common with topical structure, most likely because it is the pattern of arrangement that first comes to mind. For example, a list of bullet points is a great way to brainstorm, but if you speak from that list, your second and third points could have no relation to each other; or the last point you brainstormed should logically be first; or the third bullet is a bigger idea that, upon reflection, encompasses two other topics on your list. The end result is that the audience feels that you are jumping around between topics because there isn't a memorable or logical connection between the points. It lacks a narrative arc and could be better suited to another pattern of arrangement.

If, after careful consideration, you decide topical structure works best for your presentation, define your categories memorably (perhaps with a mnemonic device, parallel structure, or even using a metaphor or analogy); or employ Three Story Structure, which is less prone to issues with coordination and division. Consider using a purposeful method of arrangement for each of your selected stories— such as problem-solution or chronological to provide a clear narrative arc for each example you share.

Clarity

The last question to ask is do these points make sense? Take a breath, or if you can, take a day away from your presentation. Then come back and look with a fresh set of eyes and ask, will these main points make sense to my audience? Are they easy to remember (and ideally limited to two or three main points, especially in a short or technology-mediated presentation)? Sometimes our attention to detail can blind us to the most obvious and most important big-picture questions.

APPLICATION

Identify an upcoming presentation or an update you need to give in a meeting in the coming weeks. Identify two different patterns of arrangement that you could use for your main points that support your general purpose and thesis. In each arrangement, ask if the points are logically dependent or independent? In what situations would one pattern of arrangement be more helpful to listeners than the other you identified? What pattern of arrangement might be more conducive to recalling your main points while speaking or to crafting creative presentation aids?

Notes:

1. Steve Jobs, "Steve Jobs' 2005 Stanford Commencement Address," delivered on June 12, 2005. YouTube video. 15:04. https://youtu.be/UF8uR6Z6KLc. All subsequent references to Jobs' speech refer to this video.

Chapter 7

INTRODUCTIONS
AND CONCLUSIONS

Since their inception in 1984 and especially since becoming available on YouTube in 2006, TED Talks have changed the landscape of public speaking. The TED-style of presentations emphasize connection. Namely, connection between the speaker, the message, and the audience. That connection starts from the first words and is clinched with the speaker's final phrases. For speakers who are trying to make an impact, no matter how famous the person or large the audience, introductions and conclusions matter.

Consider the simple, memorable, and powerful words of Ron McCallum in the introduction of his 2013 TEDxSydney speech.

> When I was about three or four years old, I remember my Mum reading a story to me and my two big brothers. And I remember putting up my hands to feel the page of the book, to feel the picture they were discussing. And mum said, 'Darling, remember that you can't see, and you can't feel the picture, and you can't feel the print on the page.' "And I thought to myself, 'But that's what I want to do. I love stories. I want to read.' Little did I know that I'd be part of a technological revolution that would make that dream come true.[1]

Ron's listeners were hooked. No electronic gadget or mental to-do list could distract audience members from Ron's incredible explanation about the volunteers, inventors, and technologies that have revolutionized how he and other people who are visually impaired can read.

Ron led with a captivating personal story and then linked back to it in the conclusion of his presentation which brought his speech full circle. He exemplified the value of a well-crafted attention getter and clincher.

Not every presentation is a TED talk, but we'd be foolish not to take notice of what makes these presentations connect with audiences. That connection begins at the beginning and ends at the ending.

In the previous chapter, we mentioned the common misconception that if you know the material, there is little need to develop the structure of a presentation. The same mistake can happen with introductions and conclusions. Speakers can focus so intensely on the information in the main ideas that they forget they need to do some work to get their audience to those main points.

Having a clear and memorable introduction and conclusion adds interest. The law of primacy and recency states that people best remember what they hear first and last. When applied to presentations, this means you want to speak first or last in a series of speakers. Specific to the actual presentation, and more importantly, it means you want the introduction and conclusion of your presentation to shine. Here is how you can make sure they do:

Introductions

Underestimating the importance of the Attention Getter (AG) is a common mistake. Make sure that the first words out of your mouth are the most important. After all, they set the tone for your entire presentation and determine whether members of your audience will tune you in or tune you out. You do not want to wing your opening lines (another common mistake). Painstakingly develop, script, and memorize each word of your introduction. You only need a sentence or two with this level of preparation but doing so will ensure the first words out of your mouth are purposeful and powerful. This is the hook to capture your audience, give you confidence, and get your presentation off to a strong start.

Beyond an AG or hook, most effective speech introductions establish the speaker's credibility (see chapter 22 for more on ethos), position the topic as relevant and timely for listeners (see chapter 3 on analyzing the audience), articulate the thesis (see chapter 4 for more on developing one), and offer a preview of the presentation (see chapter 8 for a thorough discussion of signposting). It is easy to see why these factors would aid in communicating effectively: you

INTRODUCTIONS AND CONCLUSIONS

want the attention of audience members, you want to give them a reason to listen to you and your topic, and you want to provide a roadmap to explain how you will support that message.

For technical speeches or presentations to listeners with varying levels of experience with your subject, orienting material (basic information that the audience needs to know in order to understand your thesis) is also necessary to set the stage for the rest of your presentation. For example, if you were reporting to a credit union board of directors regarding the impact of a federal law on such financial institutions, your orienting material might include a few sentences about the history and status of the Federal Credit Union Act. Orienting material is not all of the background on a subject, but just enough to provide the most basic amount of knowledge listeners require to understand your message, or to explain an acronym or technical phrase that is important to your thesis.

Do's and Don'ts for Your AG

The following are general rules that, in the right situation, can and should be broken. When in doubt, follow these guidelines for your AG:

Do Use

Stories

Sharing an anecdote will pull your audience in. After all, everyone loves a good story. In fact, the communication theorist Walter Fisher argued humans should be called *homo narrans* because the essential difference between us and other animals is that we are storytellers. Personal stories are excellent; compelling stories about other people or dramatic hypothetical situations also work.

See for example Barack Obama's keynote address at the 2004 Democratic National Convention.

Sayings

Consider sharing a thought-provoking quotation to open a presentation. Avoid clichés and make sure to attribute the saying to the correct author. A good place to look for inspiration and to identify sources is Bartlett's Familiar Quotations.

See for example Martin Luther King, Jr.'s 1963 I Have a Dream Speech. Note: King used a concrete reference to the opening line of Lincoln's Gettysburg Address in his introduction and a direct quotation in his conclusion.

Suspense

Setting the audience up to anticipate what is coming next is an effective way to keep them engaged. Suspense can go hand-in-hand with telling a story in your speech opening. Suspense can also be achieved by asking a rhetorical question, making a promise to your audience that you'll fulfill in the course of the speech, or saying a series of seemingly disparate words or phrases and later explaining their relationship or importance.

See for example Pamela Meyer's 2011 TED Talk: How to Spot a Liar.

Shocking Information

Too many statistics or facts can bore listeners. However, a statistic that is well-documented, relevant, not-widely-known, and shocking can hook an audience in the first moments of a speech. Make sure your shocking fact or statistic is easily understandable; consider incorporating a visual aid to complement what you are saying.

See for example Joe Smith's 2012 TEDxConcordiaUPortland: How to Use a Paper Towel.

Self-Deprecating Humor

Humor isn't easy to pull off and it is not for every speaker or every occasion. It is important to note that humor is more difficult to pull off in a virtual presentation or speech delivered outside due to acoustic reasons. When people laugh in a confined space, the sound reverberates and laughter builds. The opposite happens and humor can fall flat when audience members are virtual (their microphones are muted or there is an awkward delay in the audio) or outdoors (when the laughter diffuses and sounds less robust).

However, a joke, especially one relevant to the speech topic and made at the expense of the speaker, can both grab attention and win over an audience in the beginning of a speech. Humor is a high-risk, high-reward strategy that can be particularly useful when you are persuading and need to build rapport to achieve the purpose of your speech.

See for example Dan Pink's 2009 TED Talk: The Puzzle of Motivation.

A Few Don'ts

And here are a few words of warning. Avoid these common mistakes that speakers make when starting off a speech:

Don't Use a Hackneyed Introduction Strategy

Every public-speaking instructor has heard dozens if not hundreds of student speeches that begin in these two ways:

- "Close your eyes. Imagine . . ."

- "Did you know that . . . ?"

These hackneyed introductions don't capture attention in the classroom and they don't translate well to the workplace. There are more powerful ways to open a presentation. For example, rather than awkwardly asking listeners to close their eyes and envision something, launch into a descriptive, sensory story that takes them there. Instead of starting with a rhetorical question, simply and forcefully state the shocking statistic or fact that you intend to bring to their attention.

Don't Reiterate Your Name, Speech Title, or Topic

You don't want to squander the first sentence of your speech doing something that an emcee should do for you. Script a one-minute introduction of your presentation that includes your name, a brief description of your credentials on the topic, what your audience will get from listening to you, and your speech title. Give this introduction to the event organizer or a collaborator well ahead of time. For in-person presentations, bring a hard copy for the emcee just in case. Remember, the introduction of a speaker should never be the same as the opening line of the presentation.

Don't Start by Thanking the Audience or Host

It often is appropriate and important to acknowledge event organizers, hosts, sponsors, attendees, and other dignitaries in your audience. The first sentence of your speech is not the time to do this. Hook your audience with the first sentence or two of your presentation, then say your thank-yous and continue with your introductory material.

Don't Speak Before You Command the Room

Avoid uttering a sound before you hold the floor. This may take more time for live presentations, when you make your way to the front of the room or lectern, wait for applause to end, adjust the microphone, arrange your notes, take a drink of water, and look around the room with a smile on your face. For technology-mediated communication, take a few seconds to signal a break in speakers, to ensure that you have appropriate controls in the videoconference platform, to unmute your audio, and then smile and begin speaking.

There is nothing that undercuts a speaker or shows a lack of confidence more than rushing to start. Take your time, own the room (literally or figuratively), and begin your presentation on your terms.

Don't Let "Um" Escape Your Mouth First

After you command the virtual space, don't let "um" or another filler or hesitation word slip out before you start your first sentence. The opening line of your presentation should be the most carefully rehearsed part. Ideally, it is memorized. Every word should be said slowly, crisply, and purposefully. Think through the words that should be emphasized and any gestures that would add impact. There is no room for "um" before or during a well-prepared opening line.

A corollary to this is to avoid nervous banter in your opening lines. Don't tell the audience how nervous you are, that you are a terrible public speaker, or that you are not experienced on the virtual platform, so listeners need to bear with you. In rare moments, this type of apologetic or self-deprecating comment can be used as an attention-getting strategy. But most of the time, such confessions make the speaker appear unsure, and consequently, they greatly diminish credibility.

Conclusions

Surely, the opening lines of a presentation are crucial, but don't give short shrift to the concluding lines. After all, the law of primacy and recency suggests that leaving a positive last impression is as important as making a positive first impression. The last line of any presentation should signal the end and conclude in a powerful, memorable way.

When crafting your so-called clincher, aim to return to your AG. In the case of Ron's speech, his conclusion looked to the future as well as to the past by referring to the words his mother said when he was a young boy:

> *I wonder what the future will hold. The technology will advance even further. But I can still remember my mum saying 60 years ago, "Remember darling, you'll never be able to read the print with your fingers." I'm so glad that the interaction between braille transcribers, volunteer readers, and passionate inventors has allowed this dream of reading to come true for me and blind people throughout the world.*[2]

No matter how you open your presentation, effective concluding lines often reevaluate the AG in light of the information that was communicated in the presentation. If you opened with a startling statistic—for example, the number of people in the United States who do not have access to health care—your clincher might remind the audience of this number and suggest that if they take the action you specify, that number will hopefully be zero someday. The benefit of returning to your AG in the conclusion is that it brings the presentation full circle—you are dropping off your listeners where the journey started, but with much more information than they had previously.

Oftentimes, speakers offer a call to action for their audience and use that as a clincher. The call to action is a great strategy for making a TED-style connection between the speaker, the message, and the audience, particularly for persuasive and inspirational speeches. Other presenters are drawn to sayings or quotations as a way to secure their conclusion. These can be effective, so long as the saying or quotation is not trite and is relevant to the presentation. For example, it might seem odd to end an informative briefing on pothole repairs with a quotation from Mahatma Gandhi.

No matter what you choose to do in the clincher, it is imperative that it provides a definitive and clear end to the presentation. Your conclusion should provide a clear signal to listeners that your presentation is coming to an end and help avoid awkwardness by allowing in-person attendees to clap, or the emcee or meeting facilitator to jump back in seamlessly. If you have done your job, you won't need to say "Thank you" or "That's the end" because your listeners will know unequivocally that you have concluded.

SAMPLE OPENING LINES

Dynamic speakers, including those on the TED stage, often start by sharing a captivating story in their speech introduction. Here are some tried-and-true storytelling prompts, tweeted on January 3, 2022, by business presentation expert Patricia Fripp (@PFripp), that may be useful to draw your listeners in during the opening line of your next presentation:

- "I wish you could have been there . . ."

- "I'll never forget the first (last) time . . ."

- "It was one of the most exciting days of my life . . ."

- "It was the scariest moment of my life . . ."

- "It was not exactly what I expected . . ."

APPLICATION

1. Craft or review a Sandwich Structure of an upcoming presentation—it might be something as formal as a conference speech or a webinar for prospective clients, or as informal as an update on a project that you'll give at a team meeting or an answer to a question you expect to get asked on a scheduled phone call. Brainstorm three different ways you could capture attention in the introduction. Go beyond rhetorical questions. Ask a friend or colleague which is most compelling. Use that AG in your outline and include a call back to it in your conclusion.

2. Identify a presentation you delivered recently or are crafting for an upcoming speaking role. What elements of introductions and conclusions did you include? How could you more effectively arrange those elements? Which elements could you include or exclude to improve your opening and closing?

3. In March 2014, Mellody Hobson, an American businessperson who has served as president and co-CEO of Ariel Investments as well as the chair of the board of directors of Starbucks, delivered a TED Talk titled, "Color blind or color brave?" What made her introduction powerful? Why was it so long (around 3 minutes of her 14-minute presentation)? How could she have improved her introduction? What was her call to action in the conclusion? What other elements of a conclusion might she have included to improve it? What lessons from her introduction and conclusion can you apply to your own presentations?

Notes:

1. Ron McCallum, "How Technology Allowed Me to Read," *TED*, May 4, 2013, accessed June 21, 2022, https://bit.ly/3pvbqOA

2. McCallum, "How Technology Allowed Me to Read."

Chapter 8

PREVIEWS, REVIEWS, AND TRANSITIONS

I t's unclear who first gave the sterling advice, "Tell 'em what you're gonna to tell 'em; then tell 'em; then tell 'em what you told 'em." Some say it's an adaptation of Aristotle's teachings, others that it dates to the early 1900's and comes from an Irish lawyer or an English preacher. Whoever coined the advice is less important to our purposes than following it because it still holds up in present-day speaking situations—from contributions in virtual meetings to TED Talks delivered on a stage and disseminated via YouTube.

The old saying is a reminder to offer listeners cues that communicate the structure of your presentation to audience members. As part of your introduction, the cue you provide is a clear and concise preview of your main points. In the body of your presentation, it is an overt transition between one main point and the next. And in your conclusion, it is a concrete reminder of the main points you discussed.

Previews, reviews, and transitions, also referred to as signposting, can be oral (what you say) and nonverbal (written on slides, a flip chart, or a handout). Always appropriate, signposts are particularly vital for presentations that are instructional, long, complex, or virtual because they provide a road map of the presentation to help listeners better understand, follow, and remember the message. However, they are not only helpful to listeners. Signposts can also benefit speakers who are responding to questions or contributing to meetings off the cuff by organizing thoughts, keeping the speaker on point, and avoiding tangents.

Everyone benefits from signposting, but this practice is particularly important for audience members new to a topic, those for whom English is a second language, those who have hearing loss, those who are neurodivergent, or those who are dealing with distractions as they join your presentation remotely. Much like traffic signs, you want signposts to be clear, crisp, and consistent—observable, but not so intrusive that they hurt rather than help the flow of your material.

> *Signposts should be clear, crisp, and consistent—observable, but not so intrusive that they hurt rather than help the flow of material.*

Previews

The first instance of signposting occurs after your attention getter, thank-yous, statement of speaker ethos, explanation of relevance to listeners, thesis statement, and any brief expository material (like definitions or background on a topic). This is the preview of main points. It occurs when you explicitly state the main points of your presentation. In the preview, use parallel structure to make the signpost pop. Parallel structure means that each point in the preview is constructed in the same way. Think about the number of words and the grammatical structure. For example, if you were giving an update on a project, you might offer the following as your preview: "Today, I will discuss the past, present, and future of XYZ Initiative." If you preview your main points in this way, you hope that your audience catches that your main points are:

1. Past

2. Present

3. Future

By labeling each main point as one word or a short phrase structured in parallel (such as starting with a gerund/"ing" word or starting with the same letter), the main ideas are clear and easy to recall.

A preview lets your audience know where the presentation will go; however, it is not time to expand. Over previewing can be identified by the presence of a conjunction: "because," "therefore," and "however" are a few common ones. If we take the above example, over previewing might sound like this: "Today, I will discuss the past because the story behind it is so interesting, the present, and the future, which is bright." The extra verbiage is a barrier to letting the parallelism do its job and make the preview overt and memorable.

The simpler you keep your signposts, the less awkward they will feel to deliver and the more memorable they will be to listeners. Take, for example, the opening of Steve Jobs' 2005 commencement address at Stanford University:

> *I am honored to be with you today at your commencement from one of the finest universities in the world. I never graduated from college. Truth be told, this is the closest I've ever gotten to a college graduation. Today I want to tell you three stories from my life. That's it. No big deal. Just three stories. The first story is about connecting the dots.*

He starts with a humorous hook to capture attention and establish credibility (or lack thereof), previews three stories from his life without elaborating on what they are and offers a transition to the first story he will share. Jobs provides a great example of how transitions are appropriate and useful in ceremonial speeches, just like they are appropriate and useful in conversations, responses to questions in meetings, and routine updates on projects for colleagues or clients.

Transitions

The specific type of signposting that takes place after the preview and in the body of a speech is called transitioning. From the Steve Jobs' example above, it is "The first story is about connecting the dots." This lets us know we've moved from the introduction into the first of three stories he'll share in the body of the speech. Later in the speech he says, "My second story is about love and loss." And then, "My third story is about death." These are three clear and concise transitions to introduce each of his main points.

To use a transportation metaphor, transitions are like the merging area on freeway on-ramps. It is jarring to enter a freeway with too little time to merge. Likewise, it can be jarring for a listener to move from one main idea to another without understanding the connection between the two.

Transitions can occur within one sentence, or it might take several sentences (particularly in longer presentations). Transitioning between main points of a presentation involves three elements: internal review, link, and internal preview. An internal review wraps up the previous point (often using your signpost from that point). A link connects the previous point to the next point. The link should explicitly or implicitly provide a reason why you are going to the next point. An internal preview states what the next point is. For example, when transitioning from the "past" to the "present" points in the XYZ Initiative example, one might say, "The past of XYZ Initiative dates to its inception in 2009, as a way to weather the Great Recession. As we discussed, it was a great success. That's why the company is adapting XYZ Initiative to the present, as we navigate the impacts of the COVID-19 pandemic. Specifically, we are focusing on customer engagement and online sales."

It is also important to continue to use the phrasing from the preview as you transition throughout the presentation. You might think that repeating the same words or phrases is redundant, and it is. However, the repetition is important for clarity and audience retention. If you decided to start using synonyms or change the phrasing—perhaps you signpost your second point as "developing the initiative" instead of "present" in the above example—your audience might wonder if this is part of the first point or the second. Using consistent language reduces the likelihood of such confusion. Rest assured, being repetitious is a virtue in a presenter and not a vice because listening to the spoken word requires more attention than reading a text that you can go back and reread if you are confused or distracted.

> *Being repetitious is a virtue in a presenter and not a vice because listening to the spoken word requires more attention than reading a text*

Reviews

Finally, when you have concluded the body of your speech, don't forget to signpost your main ideas once again. Presenters commonly forget the third part of, "Tell 'em what you're gonna tell 'em, tell 'em, tell 'em what you told 'em." "Tell 'em what you told 'em" means you should review the main points using the same words and phrases that will now be recognized by listeners.

In the example of the XYZ Initiative speech, the review can be as simple as, "Today, we have discussed the past, present, and future of XYZ Initiative." Keeping the wording of the review consistent at the end of your presentation will offer one last opportunity to help audience members commit your main points to memory and to signal that your speech is coming to a close. Another benefit of reviews, when done in conjunction with a clincher (see chapter 7 for more on clinchers) is that they help prevent the awkward moment at the end of a speech when listeners are not sure if a speaker has concluded and if they should wait, start clapping, ask a question, move to the next item on the meeting agenda, or do whatever is appropriate in the situation.

> *Prevent the awkward moment at the end of a speech when listeners are not sure if a speaker has concluded.*

Signposts should occur at key junctions in a presentation: after the introduction of a speech and before the first main point, between main points, and after the last main point and before the clincher. All presentations should have previews, transitions between ideas, and reviews—even short impromptu speeches. The level of detail you provide in your signposts should scale up if your presentation is long, complex, or delivered remotely. Beware of going overboard in a short, simple update or response to a question. By overdoing signposting and transitioning, you may come across as too blunt, too obvious, or too "listy." When signposting and transitioning are used together in balance with the type of presentation you are giving, signposting makes for a clear, fluid presentation for which audience members will be grateful rather than confused or frustrated.

APPLICATION

1. Think of a question you expect to get in an upcoming meeting or phone call. What simple, short signposts could you use to structure your response and make it easier for your listeners to follow? Rehearse your signposted response aloud several times until your preview, review, and transitions feel less forced and more conversational.

2. On October 24, 2009, Barack Obama delivered the first major address on health care during his presidency. Watch the speech and track its structure. What are the words or phrases that helped you identify when a new idea is being introduced? How did Obama use signposting to make a lengthy and complex speech more digestible for listeners? When could he have employed more effective signposting during the speech? Identify one section that needs better signposting and how it could be improved.

Chapter 9

PRESENTATION AIDS
AND ENGAGEMENT

A meeting is called. You and your co-workers file into a conference room or log onto a videoconference. For the next 20 minutes, the presenter reads to you from a text-laden slide deck.

When the videoconference is over you say: "That could have been an email."

This is an all-too-common scenario rooted in presentation aids that fail to *aid* the presentation. In this chapter, we will explore how to ensure that presentation aids elevate a presentation, support a dynamic delivery, and increase engagement with your audience.

By presentation aids, we are referring to software stalwarts—like Microsoft PowerPoint, Google Slides, and Apple Keynote—including numerous other new or niche presentation software platforms, as well as any analog or material items that help convey your message to your audience. Regardless of what technology or media you are using, the central question should always be: Is my presentation aid aiding my presentation?

> *Regardless of what technology or media you are using, the central question should always be: Is my presentation aid aiding my presentation?*

How you might define "aiding your presentation" can vary for each presentation you give. But if you can answer this key question in the affirmative and identify for yourself what you think is useful about your visual aids, then it is far more likely to be engaging for the audience as well.

Before we offer a few foundational principles on presentation aids, remember that presentation software should never be used as a tool for crafting presentation content. When used for content, slides become the document on which speakers script their presentation and then lifelessly read it to listeners.

To achieve a dynamic and engaging final product, start with the Sandwich Structure Method for outlining presentations. (See chapter 5.). At this point, if you decide to use slides, create a written list of graphs, charts, images, and video clips you want to design a slide for based on your Sandwich Structure Outline. Identify where these slides dovetail with the outline, noting if and where you should include slides that indicate signposting (preview, review, and transitions) to help listeners follow the structure of the presentation.

Now that we've addressed process, let's get to the foundational principles of presentation aids:

Presentation Aids Are a Choice

You as the presenter have some choice in your presentation aids. The degree of choice may vary. You might have the choice as to whether or not you use them at all. There are fields and professions where it might seem as though you do not have a choice. Do not assume you have to use slides. Bucking industry or event norms on the use of presentation aids might feel uncomfortable, but rejecting slides in favor of a prop, whiteboard, or nothing at all could help you stand out as a presenter and make your message more memorable.

It might be the case that you are required to submit slides as a condition of presentation. In those instances, you still have some say as to what material is presented, how much is presented, how you explain it to the audience, and how the presentation is timed. Own that choice so that you feel confident in what you are showing your audience.

Some presentations are standardized. Sales professionals may speak from the same set of pitch decks. Financial or legal professionals may be limited to slides that are pre-approved by compliance officers. Officials at a government agency and advocates at a non-profit may use the same slides to give informational presentations to various stakeholders. If you find yourself in this situation, then take the time to review the slides so that you feel (and your audience feels) that the presentation aids are a purposeful and meaningful choice. Give yourself agency to spend longer on slides more relevant to a particular audience and skip over irrelevant slides entirely.

Choices about presentation aids should change depending on the speaking situation. At a table-top briefing where a speaker is delivering a presentation to several people in person at the same table, using presentation software would be awkward at best. At worst, it would hinder the ability to build rapport and engage in meaningful dialogue. The same presentation delivered remotely to listeners who are each joining via a videoconferencing platform might hold attention longer and garner more questions from listeners if the speaker shared their screen to display a specific chart or image at a few key moments in the briefing.

Presentation Aids Should Supplement, Not Replace the Presenter

If a listener can get everything he or she needs from the screen or a handout, then you, the presenter, have reduced your value and utility. This goes back to the situation that opened this chapter and also recalls the question, "Why am I Speaking?" that was posed in chapter 3. If the slide deck says it all, why not just send it to everyone to read on their own? If you read text from your visual aids with no additions, audience members can tune you out and not miss a thing. At this point, you have effectively made yourself obsolete and created competition for the attention of listeners. Worse yet, you likely insulted your audience members by assuming they need someone to read aloud to them and by wasting their valuable time.

Instead, use presentation aids to elevate the presentation. They should help listeners understand and remember your message. For example, if you are discussing the buying trends over the last five years, the numbers could get overwhelming if presented only orally. A simple, well-labeled, and descriptive line graph would provide the means for audience members to see and grasp your point immediately. If you are establishing your credibility as an architect, it would make your case more memorable, interesting, and believable if you showed several images of plans you drew and buildings constructed using them. Images complement the verbal aspect of your speech to make your presentation more concrete and memorable.

If you decide to use presentation software, think of it as a relatively easy and effective way to curate visual aids. There is always the possibility that you might run into technological difficulties (and Murphy's law says you will), but when such programs work as intended, they are a fantastic way to project graphs, charts, diagrams, photographs, pictures, and video clips for a large audience to see. One advantage of online presentations is that videoconference platforms have robust screen sharing features that work reliably and consistently, unlike in-person presentations where problems with internet connectivity and AV compatibility are common.

Presentation Aids Are for the Audience, Not the Speaker

As we mentioned at the outset of this chapter, avoid making the mistake of using slides as your notes. You certainly can and should use a Sandwich Structure Outline to speak from, but these materials should never be available to listeners on a screen or on a handout. And if you must provide a client or listener a stand-alone report that your presentation is based on or document for future reference with a list of legal precedents or technical instructions, create a separate set of slides for your oral presentation. Rest assured, the presentation you speak from does not have to be the same as the handout, document, or written report you provide listeners. On the contrary, it can be useful to think of presentation aids as a supplement to a written document that is meant to breathe life, through videos, pictures, and stories, into the facts and data on paper or slides for a report created using presentation software. Remember, using presentation software to develop a written document does not mean that the product is a presentation appropriate for oral delivery.

> *Remember, using presentation software to develop a written document does not mean that the product is a presentation appropriate for oral delivery.*

When selecting presentation aids to include in your next speech, ask yourself: Does this presentation aid provide something that could not be conveyed with words alone? Is there a story that would come alive or a piece of information that would make more sense if paired with a presentation aid? Would a change in modality, such as the use of a whiteboard, image, or video, help focus the attention of listeners at this point in the presentation? If you answered yes, include it. If you are including the presentation aid because it will serve as a prompt for what you want to say, leave it out.

GENERAL GUIDELINES FOR SLIDE COMPOSITION

1. White is for background
2. Text is for labeling
3. Images are for storytelling

Presentation Aids Should Be Simple and Sophisticated

The most used website globally is Google. The logo is rendered as large text of the site name (often artistically rendered to honor a person or occasion) on a sea of white with a search box beneath it. Speakers would be well served to use it as inspiration for their own slide design guidelines.

Color

Consider how the use of color impacts the ability to read content. Putting yellow, orange, or red text on a white slide renders the text virtually invisible. And white text on a black or dark background is also very difficult to read. Black or dark text on a white or light background is standard fare and a best practice for inclusion because it is easy to read. And, if you need to print slides, this format will save you a lot of toner.

Composition

Each type of presentation software has its own selection of templates and slide themes. Check with your organization or an event organizer regarding a preferred or required presentation software or template. If you are choosing one, remember that it should be appropriate for the situation (your purpose, the audience, or the situation). Picking something "cute" might be fun for a friend's birthday party or the boss's roast but should not be the standard for everyday business (unless you are in the business of cute).

The second dimension of composition is words on the page (or slide as it were). Ideally, text should be used for labeling visual information or for signposting key ideas. If you must include a list of key ideas, a common rule for composing text on a single presentation slide is the 5x5 Rule: Have no more than five bullet points, and each point should be no more than five words long. This rule of thumb discourages both cut-and-pasting as well as the use of slides as speaking notes rather than as a tool to help listeners understand and remember. Whenever possible, make effective use of the few words that do appear on your visual aids. Instead of describing what is on the slide, make a claim that helps listeners understand that take-away message. For example, instead of labeling a slide: "Sales trends across locations," you could write: "Sales skyrocketing in the Midwest."

The 5x5 Rule is a guideline rather than a hard and fast policy. Not only can it be broken, but if it will make your slide more effective, you are encouraged to break it carefully and thoughtfully. Think carefully about how to make your slide effective. If, for example, you wanted to quote five sentences from an external reviewer's report of your organization, you would not place that text on a slide and then instruct your audience to read it while you talk. This forces a choice between you and the visuals, often leading to an unintended third consequence of the audience deciding to tune out. Instead, you could read the first sentence aloud. Then, paraphrase the next four sentences, providing enough time in your paraphrasing for the audience to read the rest of the paragraph. By guiding your audience through the presentation aid, you can use the information to its fullest potential while also maintaining the attention of your audience.

Lastly, protect white space. Like the homepage for Google, you want your slides to be crisp, simple, and singular. Avoid filling them up with too much stuff. Less is more when it comes to visuals.

Coordination

It goes without saying that the presentation aid should hang together as a cohesive whole. There is rarely a reason to infuse a different design scheme, font, color, animation, etc. into the middle of a presentation. It would not coordinate with the rest of the presentation and would only serve to interrupt the flow. This problem is usually an unintended consequence of having multiple people crafting visual aids for a single presentation. Make sure there is a process by which slides, handouts, etc. are reviewed and updated for consistency in design, formatting, and even capitalization and punctuation.

Presentation Aids, Like All Parts of a Presentation, Need to be Rehearsed

Let's cover the basics of successfully incorporating presentation aids:

Practice

Whether you are using presentation software in person or via videoconference, a poster, a prop, or other material to supplement your speech, you must practice with it. Start incorporating your presentation aids during your early rehearsals so you can use them confidently, fluidly, and automatically. See chapter 17 on rehearsals. There is nothing worse than fumbling through a demonstration or finishing a presentation only to realize that you forgot to advance your slides or display the objects you intended to show. If you don't rehearse, it is easy to get flustered or forget in the moment when nerves are running high. If you do rehearse, you might find that you develop muscle memory with the visual aids, such that you end up taking fewer and fewer glances at your Sandwich Structure Outline.

Make sure you do a technical rehearsal using the IT setup several days ahead of time. For in-person presentations, check that your computer and slides are compatible with the AV system. Acquaint yourself with the buttons on the clicker and where to point it to advance slides.

For online speaking roles, get comfortable sharing your screen, advancing slides, playing video clips, and interacting with the audience. Note that some features (such as slide animation, video clips, breakout rooms, and whiteboards) do not function in every videoconference and webinar platform; you may need to reformat slides or use different functionality to achieve your goals. It is best to identify this well in advance and not during a technology check completed 15 minutes before you start your presentation. Also, make sure to update your videoconference platform software and computer operating system before and not after your dress rehearsal!

Don't Let Slides Become a Distraction

You certainly don't want to advance a slide too soon, but the opposite problem is more common: speakers keep a visual aid displayed past the point of usefulness. In the case of presentation software, this means leaving text or an image on the screen after you move on to another point. When a visual doesn't sync with the spoken word, listeners can become distracted. A good practice is to advance to a relevant slide or add a black placeholder slide to help focus the attention of listeners. For virtual presentations, you can even turn off the screen share function until you are ready to display your next image.

Make Sure Presentation Aids are Expendable

We all know from personal experience that technology will fail at some point. Perhaps you forgot a power cord for your laptop, or the internet connection is unstable, or your client's IT security firewall does not allow use of videos you carefully embedded in your slides. No matter how conscientious you are, at some point, something can and will go wrong with your virtual platform or presentation aids. As important as a presentation aid and videoconference platform might be to your speech, it is important to consider what you would do if you did not have it. Make sure you have backup plans (like sharing slides with an event planner or producer beforehand) as well as a contingency plan for giving the speech without the presentation aid (that may mean sending your listeners a PDF of your slides and talking them through via a teleconference call). After all, the show must go on. The hallmark of expert speakers is the ability to proceed with grace and confidence in the face of technological failures such that audience members may never know there was a problem in the first place.

APPLICATION

1. Watch the following two TED Talks that use very different types of visual aids: 1) "The Beauty of Data Visualization," by David McCandless in 2010; and 2) "Population Growth, Box by Box," by Hans Rosling in 2010. How do visuals enhance each presenter's argument? What are the main lessons about using visuals to represent complex ideas?

2. Craft a five-minute descriptive speech that paints for listeners a vivid picture of a person, place, or thing. Deliver and record your speech three times: once using presentation software, once using a non-electronic presentation aid (poster, picture, prop, etc.), and once with no presentation aids. Review the recordings. How did your delivery differ? What were the strengths and weaknesses of using electronic presentation aids, non-electronic presentation aids, and no presentation aids?

CHECKLIST FOR PRESENTATION CONTENT

You are doing the hard work of crafting a great presentation. Before you start rehearsing. Here is a checklist for reviewing and refining your content. Aim to answer with all yeses.

THE BIG PICTURE

- ☐ Did you start by analyzing the audience and occasion?

- ☐ Did you identify the topic and speech purpose based on the analysis of audience and situation?

- ☐ Did you start crafting content on one piece of paper or one page on a word-processing platform oriented horizontally or with our online Sandwich Structure Tool?

THE WORDS

- ☐ Did you use words and phrases on the Sandwich Structure and only script the introductory and concluding lines?

- ☐ Does the thesis on your outline state a clear position? Test this by adding "I believe . . . " to the start of your thesis. It should make sense.

- ☐ Does the presentation have a logical structure and narrative arc?

- ☐ Does that speech structure support your purpose (e.g. informative or persuasive)?

- ☐ Do main points achieve balance, clarity, and parallel structure?

- ☐ Does the scripted introduction have an attention getter, make the topic timely and relevant, establish speaker credibility, and include necessary orienting material or thank yous?

- ☐ Does the scripted conclusion include needed thank yous and a clear call to action, as well as a clincher that links concretely to the attention-getter in the introduction?

THE VISUALS

☐ Does the outline include visual cues to remind the speaker to preview, review, and transition the main points?

☐ Did you craft slides based on the outline to highlight the presentation structure, to display images that make stories more concrete, and to give visual representations of data cited?

☐ Did you limit text on slides to key words, phrases, and labels?

☐ Do the slides supplement rather than replace the speaker?

☐ Did you limit the length of the overall presentation to 20 minutes or include engagement techniques and changes in modality (e.g. different speakers and video clips) at least that often for in-person presentations and more often for online or hybrid formats?

CHECKLIST FOR INTRODUCTIONS AND CONCLUSIONS

In the content section of this book, we have explored components of excellent content. It's important to understand how those components combine to create an effective introduction and conclusion.

INTRODUCTIONS SHOULD:

- ☐ Start with an attention getter to get listeners interested. (See chapter 7 on attention getters.)

- ☐ Give listeners a reason to care. The introduction should position the topic as timely and relevant.

- ☐ Establish the credibility of the speaker. This can be accomplished by a passing comment about experience working on an issue or a more in-depth biographical sketch. The familiarity of audience members with the speaker should inform these choices, as well as the appropriateness of including a formal speech introduction.

- ☐ Clarify the thesis statement. (See chapter 4 on topic and thesis.)

- ☐ Preview the main points. (See chapter 8 on previews.)

- ☐ Show gratitude to the event organizer, sponsor, host, dignitaries, etc. as appropriate to the situation.

- ☐ Provide orienting material, such as definitions or a brief history of a project or issue, as needed.

- ☐ Include reminders about a code of conduct or instructions on how to submit questions during the presentation, as needed.

Every introduction should start with an attention getter. Reciting your presentation title, name, or thesis should never be the first words out of your mouth, even if you are delivering a brief update during a routine meeting. The attention getter can be short and to the point, but you should have a hook to reel in listeners.

The statement of relevance and timeliness, information on speaker credibility, thesis, preview, as well as thank yous and orienting material (as needed) do not need to be delivered in a prescribed order. They can be incorporated in whatever manner is most logical and conversational.

CONCLUSIONS SHOULD:

- ☐ Mention housekeeping items, such as thanking event organizers again, reminding audience members to complete an evaluation, or instructing conference attendees where they should go next.

- ☐ Review main points. (See chapter 8 on reviews.)

- ☐ Repeat the thesis statement.

- ☐ Include a call to action, if the speaker wants audience members to do something specific like cast a vote, book a consultation, sign a proposal, or approve a budget. It is always a good idea to consider whether a call to action is merited, but having one in a conclusion is not always necessary. (See chapter 22 on Monroe's Motivated Sequence.)

- ☐ End with a clincher. This should refer concretely and unequivocally to the concept introduced in the attention getter. (See chapter 7 on clinchers.)

Again, the order of elements in a conclusion is flexible. Ideally, the clincher should be the last line so it is clear that the presenter has come full circle to the attention getter. Putting the attention getter too early in the conclusion can make the end of a presentation less memorable, forceful, and impactful.

Chapter 10

THE SIX ELEMENTS OF EXECUTIVE PRESENCE AND AUTHENTICITY

Sylvia Ann Hewlett, author of *Executive Presence: The Missing Link Between Merit and Success*, provides a useful definition:

> *Executive presence is the 'it factor,' a heady combination of confidence, poise, and authenticity that convinces the rest of us we are in the presence of someone who's going places. [...] Executive presence is not just a measure of performance. Rather, executive presence is a measure of image: whether you signal to others that you 'have what it takes,' that you are leadership material.[1]*

If executive presence is a measure of image rather than performance, does it really matter? Shouldn't our content stand on its own regardless of how we deliver it?

We absolutely believe that executive presence matters, and we also wish that it didn't matter as much as it does. Listeners make judgments, many subconsciously, regarding content based on the way it is delivered. It can be difficult to understand a message that is delivered too quickly, too quietly, or with too many distractions. Similarly, when writing a report or memo, your ideas may be considered less competent and compelling if rules of grammar are ignored and more confusing if your message is conveyed with typos and formatting issues.

> *Listeners make judgments regarding content based on the way it is delivered.*

Just as you can improve as a writer and consciously decide to break the conventions of writing to convey your authentic voice as an author, you should understand what communication behaviors have become associated with confident speaking and make purposeful decisions about which ones to adopt or to reject.

Since the time of ancient Greek rhetoricians, the "rules" of public speaking and elocution have been written by men in positions of power. Such "rules" disadvantage marginalized people, limit the diversity of voices that have credibility in the public sphere, and can discourage authentic communication.

Our goal for exploring executive presence is not to prescribe the rules of executive presence or to make every professional look and sound the same. Rather, our goal is to raise awareness of communication behaviors that have become associated with confident speaking; to invite professionals to consider which of the behaviors they can authentically engage in and which they can address to improve their effectiveness; to give speakers a toolkit of skills to draw on as they make purposeful decisions based on the risks and rewards of authenticity in various communication situations; and to encourage us all to be more authentic as speakers and inclusive of different styles of speaking as listeners.

Two nuances of executive presence must be acknowledged before diving into its components. First, executive presence is not only relevant to public speaking situations. Whether you realize it or not, you are constantly presenting at work when you are speaking to one person on the phone, at the proverbial water cooler, to a small group during a meeting or business lunch, or to hundreds or thousands of listeners at a conference or on a webinar. Elevating your presence in routine and low-risk situations will provide valuable experience needed to succeed in higher-risk and higher-profile speaking roles. Second, executive presence is not only relevant to executives. Conveying confidence while communicating is crucial at every career level—if you are a student in school; a recent graduate networking and interviewing for jobs; an early career professional building your personal brand; a mid-career professional speaking up in or leading meetings and delivering briefings; or a seasoned professional who is pitching clients, training colleagues, providing feedback, making recommendations, and delivering speeches.

If executive presence is important to all professionals, should it be called executive presence? Perhaps it would be better termed "professional presence" or "leadership presence" or "communication presence." No matter what you call it, you can convey confidence and improve communication outcomes in any workplace speaking situation at any stage of your career by focusing on your stance, sound, smile, silence, sight, and setup. Following is an overview of each of these speaking proficiencies, the six S's, which will be expanded upon in the subsequent six chapters.

Stance

The guiding principles of effective body language are to take-up physical space and avoid distracting movements. It may seem obvious, but is worth emphasizing, that in computer-mediated communication situations you should use video and turn on your camera whenever possible and especially when speaking to provide physical presence. It is easy for listeners to forget you exist when they can't see you.

> *In computer-mediated communication situations, turn on your camera whenever possible and especially when speaking to provide physical presence.*

Whenever you are given the option to stand to present during in-person situations, take it. For panels you moderate or online speeches where you get to curate the setup, make standing an option. Standing takes up more physical space than sitting which enhances executive presence. While standing, plant yourself firmly. Keep your feet glued to the ground about hip-distance apart with weight equally distributed on the legs. Imagine that your feet are set in concrete to prevent rocking, swaying, tapping, or pacing. It is fine to move across a room or a stage purposefully but plant your feet between moves. Make sure you stay consistently in the camera view if you have a hybrid audience so your online listeners can always see you. Adhere painter's tape to the floor to mark your speaking area in these situations.

Next, sit or stand tall and open your posture. Roll your shoulders back, engage your core, and raise your chest expanding the area from your hips to your shoulders. Maintain upward energy and avoid hunching by pretending there's a string attached from the crown of your head to the ceiling. Excellent posture conveys confidence before a single word is spoken.

Also, let your hands hang at your sides in a neutral position between gestures while standing, and rest them on the table or at your lap while sitting. This helps prevent mindlessly "talking with the hands" or making repetitive motions with them at your waist. Purposeless movement distracts listeners from your message and is a sign of nervousness.

Sound

If you want to sound confident and have vocal presence, your voice must be easily audible. This starts with excellent posture (hence standing or sitting in a firm chair) and speaking from the diaphragm (not the throat). Aim to speak in the low end of your natural range, at a slow rate, and crisply; all are best practices but particularly useful in computer-mediated formats that have been developed and optimized for lower vocal tones and which have the propensity to distort and freeze. Remember to speak louder than you think you should. After all, you likely never have left an event thinking: "That speaker was just too loud!"

> *Remember to speak louder than you think you should.*

While your computer's built-in camera is generally sufficient for video, computer audio is a different story. At the very least, use an earbud-microphone combo to participate in online meetings and events. To facilitate meetings or deliver an online speech, invest in a higher-quality external microphone. For hybrid speaking roles, test equipment with AV professionals ahead of time to ensure both online and in-person listeners can hear easily.

Smile

A smile is best understood as an effort by speakers to present with energy and enthusiasm—no matter how routine or somber their subject. Even serious professionals talking about serious topics look more assured when they have a "bright" face—a slight lift of the eyes, cheeks, and corners of the mouth. A soft smile not only makes your voice more pleasant to listen to, but it also disguises any nervousness you may be experiencing and makes you appear friendly and approachable. You want to use other facial expressions when delivering unwelcome news so there is never a conflict between your verbal and nonverbal communication. For good news, neutral information, or technical topics, throw on a smile. And remember in virtual meetings, everyone can see your face in the attendee gallery even when you are not speaking! So, maintain that soft smile when you are listening too.

Silence

When speakers avoid pauses, it often results in sentences that are littered with junk words, such as "um," "ah," "you know," "kind of," "like," "so," and "well." These vocal fillers make you appear unpolished, unprepared, and unprofessional. Used in excess, they can be distracting and even undermine your credibility. One effective strategy to reduce junk words is to put your lips together briefly where there are commas and periods in your speaking or when you are thinking of your next thought, as these are places when filler words often creep in—you can't articulate a junk word when your lips are together.

Sight

Lasting eye contact is crucial for building rapport with listeners and conveying confidence as a speaker. When speaking in person, hold your gaze on an audience member for three full seconds—likely longer than you think you should. Then move on and hold your gaze on someone else in a different part of the room. Sustained and direct eye contact builds rapport by giving audience members the feeling that they are engaged in an intimate conversation.

> *Lasting eye contact is crucial for building rapport with listeners and conveying confidence as a speaker.*

This skill is particularly difficult in virtual presentations because you need to position your equipment properly and stare into a camera lens to give virtual listeners the experience of receiving eye contact. It is counterintuitive, but if you look at the eyes of listeners in the videoconference gallery on your computer screen, you won't give them the experience of eye contact. It will look like you are reading a script. To support effective eye contact with the camera, position your camera at eye level and consider a reminder to look at it (such as a Post-It Note with an arrow pointing at the camera or one that reads, "Look here!"). For hybrid presentations, make sure you know where the camera is located so you can treat it as a VIP audience member. Look directly into the camera lens at regular intervals, and especially when you are directly addressing online audience members.

Setup

For in-person presentations, the setting and technology available are generally dictated for you—in the board room at your office, the breakout room at the conference where you are speaking on a panel, the auditorium where your speech will take place, or the assigned office or cubicle at your place of work. However, it can be improved by requesting a microphone for any meeting larger than a small table so everyone can hear; being strategic about where you sit during meetings; what you wear when presenting; and curating your office workspace (if you have one) to optimize your setup for virtual meetings and events (as they will likely still occur even if you are working in an office building fulltime).

For online presentations, the first step is to make sure you have a strong Internet connection, an up-to-date computer operating system and videoconference platform, a serviceable camera, and a robust microphone. Next, spruce up your background. Although you don't need to create a fancy studio backdrop when participating in virtual meetings, you should curate an uncluttered, professional setting that is as free of distractions as possible. If this is not possible, enable the blurred background feature if your videoconference platform offers one. For formal presentations, upgrade to a high-quality microphone and a thoughtfully curated backdrop or a greenscreen and custom virtual background.

For hybrid speaking events, online participants will not have the exact same experience as in-person participants, but they can and should have a quality experience that does not relegate them to second-class status. This requires planning and testing to ensure online participants can see and hear the presenter and their materials, and that online attendees are thoughtfully included and can be seen and heard when they participate.

By exploring the six elements of executive presence in online, hybrid, and in-person speaking situations, namely stance, sound, smile, silence, sight, and setup, you can start becoming more aware of your communication behaviors, understanding the impact of those behaviors, and making purposeful decisions about which behaviors you must authentically embrace and which you can tweak to convey more confidence and improve communication outcomes.

APPLICATION

1. Get a recording of a presentation you deliver in a meeting, panel discussion, training program, or conference presentation. These situations are often and easily recorded in videoconference platforms—you may already have a recent recording, or you can ask attendees if you can hit record at the start of an upcoming event during which you are presenting. Watch the recording and inventory your executive presence, paying close attention to the six S's (stance, sound, smile, silence, sight, and setup). What are your greatest strengths? What jumped out at you as areas needing improvement?

2. Watch a recording of a speaker you admire or a TED Talk that looks interesting. Inventory the speaker's executive presence, playing close attention to the six S's. Which proficiencies are strengths of the speaker? Which could they improve upon? What "rules" did the speaker break and how did it influence your judgments about the speaker's authenticity, the content, or your ability to understand the message?

Notes:

1.   Sylvia Ann Hewlett, *Executive Presence: The Missing Link between Merit and Success* (New York: Harper Collins, 2014).

Chapter 11

STANCE

In the previous chapter, we mentioned that listers make judgments about speakers, many subconsciously, about content based on the way it is delivered. Many of those judgments are based on posture and body movement before a presenter even says a word.

In her 2015 book *Presence: Bringing Your Boldest Self to Your Biggest Challenges*, Amy Cuddy asserted, "Expansive, open body language is closely tied to dominance across the animal kingdom, including humans, other primates, dogs, cats, snakes, fish, and birds, and many other species. When we feel powerful, we make ourselves bigger."[1] As it pertains to presenting, taking up physical space is an important way to convey confidence. This chapter will provide suggestions to help speakers improve their executive presence by taking up more vertical and horizontal space as well as by avoiding distracting movements with the body. The suggestions will start from the ground and work their way up from the feet.

Lower Body

Keep your feet planted and hip distance apart. Legs that are close together or crossed make your body appear smaller. To check that your feet truly are at hip distance, jump in the air and pretend that you are catching a ball (such as a dodgeball or basketball). Notice where your feet land and how far apart they are; this is where they should be positioned during standing presentations.

Keep your feet firmly planted on the ground—as if set in concrete. Avoid pacing, dancing, tapping, crossing of your feet, or rocking up on your toes. Also, avoid popping a hip or shifting weight from one side to the other. Such movements can be distracting. Focus on adopting a wide, still stance and controlling your body before adding movement to different parts of your speaking area or the room. This helps ensure that foot movement is purposeful, rather than a manifestation of nervous energy.

When ready, move in the speaking area to show movement from one key idea to the next. For example, you might stand at a lectern for the introduction of your speech, move to the right-hand side of the speaking area to talk about your first main point, walk to the left-hand side of the speaking area while transitioning to the next point, deliver your second main point there, and return to the lectern for your conclusion. This harmonizes your movement with the speech, and subtly cues listeners to the structure of and transitions in your presentation. For hybrid speaking situations, make sure you consistently stay in the camera view so online listeners can always see you. Use painter's tape on the floor to mark the speaking area in these situations.

If you are speaking from a lectern, do not stand behind it. It obscures your body and reduces your physical presence. Instead, stand next to the lectern so listeners can see you, but you can still see your notes. If you have a lavalier microphone, consider moving away from the lectern and closer to your audience to enhance your physical presence.

KNOW THE DIFFERENCE BETWEEN A LECTERN AND A PODIUM

All too often used interchangeably, a lectern is a stand used to support a text in a convenient position for a standing speaker, whereas a podium is the platform on which a presenter stands while delivering a speech.

A speaker puts notes on the lectern and stands on the podium. It helps to remember the root word "pod" means foot (as in podiatrist). You put your feet on a podium, not a lectern. A lectern is where you put lecture notes.

Even though listeners don't see your lower body during virtual communication, you should still have your feet planted on the ground. Unnecessary lower-body movements while sitting or standing may be audible or discernable on camera, serving to detract from your physical presence and message.

If you would stand during the in-person version of a presentation, arrange your computer, camera, and microphone so you can stand up to deliver it online. Standing can increase your level of energy and ability to project your voice. If you would normally sit during a meeting or tabletop briefing, feel free to sit in a firm chair to deliver it virtually. Avoid chairs that swivel or roll, as they can introduce distracting movements.

Hands

If you are like many presenters, you might wonder what to do with your hands. Avoid crossing them in front of your chest or clasping them at your waist because those postures take-up less space horizontally and reduce physical presence. For seated remarks, rest hands on the table. This is preferred because it makes it easier to use your hands to gesture and it helps keep your posture straight. Placing the hands under the table hides them and can make it easier to slouch. If there is no table, loosely rest your hands on your lap.

Before

After

Spoken with Authority Coach Bjørn Stillion Southard with hands under table and hands on table.

Photos courtesy of Bjørn Stillion Southard.

For standing remarks, let your hands hang naturally at your sides between purposeful and impactful gestures. Keeping hands loosely at your sides might take some getting used to, but other hand placements can have negative connotations. For example, crossing the arms over the chest can convey defensiveness; putting the hands on the hips can come across as bossy or matter-of-fact; placing hands in pants pockets can lead to the clanking of contents or shoulders that are raised too high; clasping the hands in front of the body can be read as nervous, closed off, or insecure; and, holding the hands behind the back can look as if the speaker is trying to hide something. In addition to conveying undesirable or unintended meanings, such positions can prevent speakers from gesturing in purposeful, memorable ways that fill physical space. Pay attention to the hand placement of stage actors and keynote speakers. They often present with their hands hanging loosely at their sides between gestures. You will notice that the position seems natural and neutral. Rest assured it feels more awkward to you than it will look to others.

Avoid "T-Rex arms" where your upper arms are glued to your body and you make small, frantic gestures with your hands at chest level. Instead, initiate gestures from the elbows and take-up horizontal space, especially for in-person presentations with larger audiences. Move slowly to take-up temporal space and to communicate calmness. When motioning with the hands, keep the fingers together (no finger wagging or pointing) and palms up (which are more welcoming than palms down). Make sure purposeful gestures are visible and not behind a lectern, under a table, or outside the frame of your camera for computer-mediated communication.

Many speakers make the mistake of moving their hands in a distracting manner (e.g., constantly talking with the hands, tapping fingers on a desk, or clicking a pen). These are often manifestations of nervous energy rather than purposeful movements that add meaning to a presentation. They may also be self-soothing or self-stimulatory behaviors, also called stimming, which neurodivergent and neurotypical humans engage in to reduce anxiety or respond to a need for physical movement. Having awareness of such behaviors may help presenters engage in them less frequently or transition to less distracting behaviors (from clicking a pen to squeezing a stress-relief ball or spinning the outer rung of a "worry ring" piece of jewelry for example).

When gesturing on a videoconference call or webinar, keep your hands high and tight. Gestures must be no wider than your shoulders to appear in the camera view and must be close to your shoulder-height so your hands don't obscure your face.

Upper Body

Think about utilizing space with your upper body. Remember to stand or sit as tall as possible. One way to achieve more vertical energy and height is to imagine a string attached to the crown of your head that is being pulled toward the ceiling. The crown of your head should go higher, making you taller. Tuck your chin (and avoid raising it) as if someone pushed it toward your chest. Sitting in a firm chair will make it easier to take-up vertical space in a seated position.

To take-up space horizontally with your upper body, relax the shoulders, roll them down your back, and open across your chest. Hunched shoulders take-up less space and signal insecurity; tense shoulders indicate nervousness and cause you to speak in a high pitch and at a fast pace. Rolling the shoulders back promotes a proud chest, meaning that the chest is both open and lifted. This upper-body posture not only conveys confidence by taking up horizontal space, but it is also conducive to projecting the voice properly from the diaphragm and not from the throat. (See chapter 12 for more on sound.)

From the soles of your feet to the crown of your head, these guidelines for stance will enhance your physical presence and convey confidence before you say a word in any speaking situation.

TURN ON YOUR CAMERA

It may seem obvious, but to convey confidence nonverbally, listeners must see the speaker.

When speaking in technology-mediated communication situations, use a videoconference platform instead of a telephone, turn on your camera (especially when speaking), sit close to it, and frame yourself so listeners can see you from the chest up. If you printed a photo of your image and drew horizontal lines across the screen ⅓ from the top and ⅓ from the bottom, the lines should be roughly at eye level and chin level when you are sitting close enough and framed properly.

Example

Spoken with Authority Coach Michele Morrissey positioned with her eyes at the top ⅓ and chin at the bottom ⅓ of the screen.

Photo courtesy of Michele Morrissey.

Application

1. Record yourself three times practicing an upcoming presentation or contribution to a meeting. On the first recording, stand and gesture as you naturally would. On the second, focus on improving your posture and standing still with your hands at your sides in a neutral position throughout the entire recording. The third time, maintain your improved posture, add three purposeful and impactful gestures, and keep your hands at your sides in a neutral position between those gestures.

    Review the three recordings. What movements did you make in the first recording that might have been distracting to listeners? How successfully were you able to stand completely still in the second? How did that make you feel? How did it impact the authenticity of your delivery? How did your gestures impact the third rendition of your story? How did your stance improve over the three recordings? How can you continue to take-up more physical space and use purposeful and interesting movements, while also honoring your authenticity as a speaker?

2. Watch a recording of a speaker you admire or a TED Talk that looks interesting. Inventory the speaker's physical presence, playing close attention to posture, body language, and hand movements. How did the speaker utilize space horizontally and vertically? How did specific body movements enhance or detract from their message? How did the speaker's body language impact their ability to convey confidence and connect with audience members? How can you apply what you learned in this analysis to your next presentation?

Note:

1.   Amy Cuddy, *Presence: Bringing Your Boldest Self to Your Biggest Challenges* (New York: Little, Brown and Company, 2015).

Chapter 12

SOUND

Americans have tended to evaluate speakers in terms of their sustained eye contact, absence of filler words (e.g., like, ummm, so), and an energetic voice. There is research to support the significance of the sound of a speaker's voice in audience evaluation of that speaker.

A 2013 study asked experts and lay listeners to evaluate over one-hundred business executive speeches. The study observed that the vocal quality of the speech accounted for 23 percent of the audience evaluation of the speeches. This means that nearly one-quarter of comments about the speeches—positive and negative—mentioned some element of sound. By comparison, content accounted for 11 percent of the evaluation.[1] We do not claim that this ratio is the same for every audience and every speaker, and many would argue it ought not be the case. Nevertheless, research and experience tell us that the sound of your voice matters.

> *The sound of your voice matters.*

A few caveats are important to mention before discussing some key elements of sound.

First, we aim to help you make your voice the best version of *your voice*, not change who you are. This perspective helps reduce the anxiety that we experience when we feel like an impostor. It also allows for the unique qualities of you as a person to come through. If we all wanted to hear the same kind of speaker, we'd program a robot to do that. What a boring world it would be.

Second, we believe that speakers can help educate and train audiences to hear different kinds of voices as credible and powerful. Of course, there are situational, organizational, and cultural norms that speakers must be aware of. However, there are many norms that are passively accepted that should be looked at with an open mind.

These caveats aside, the following topics can provide points of reference as you hone the sound of your voice.

Volume

First and foremost, speakers must project. If you are not heard, your message will not get across, nor will any "shades of deeper meaning," for that matter.

Always speak louder than you think you should. Speaking loudly is a sign of confidence. Even in a one-on-one job interview, a meeting, or in situation when you have a microphone available, use a louder volume than you would in an everyday conversation. This ensures that your voice is forceful, that it doesn't quiver, and that it doesn't come across as weak.

As the room and audience get larger, your volume must scale up as well. When you are speaking in a conference room or classroom without access to a microphone, you should be speaking in a raised voice, almost yelling, and should feel the sound of your voice resonating in your upper chest. Your voice will feel tired after projecting in this manner, so make sure to drink plenty of water and rest your voice before and after such speaking situations.

To project effectively, work on opening your chest and midsection; stand tall, lift your chest, and roll your shoulders back and down the shoulder blades. Think of filling the entire room with sound—you might visualize your voice as red paint that you are trying to spray on the back wall of the room in which you are presenting. When you project your voice, focus on speaking from the diaphragm, not the throat (this prevents damage to your vocal cords).

TECHNOLOGY

A good place to start improving your vocal presence is by having serviceable audio equipment and using it properly. Whenever possible in online communication, use an external microphone rather than the one built into your computer. (See chapter 16 for more on setup.) If you regularly participate in videoconferences or if you facilitate meetings or webinars, you should invest in a high-quality microphone and a pop filter (a shield that goes in front of the microphone to enhance audio quality, especially of "p" and "b" sounds). For a high-tech external microphone, check that it is on the correct setting, usually cardioid for public speaking. Run your videoconference platform's audio test feature to check sound quality before you join the meeting.

For in-person and hybrid speaking roles that have more attendees than fit around a conference table, request and use a microphone. Do a sound check with AV professionals to get comfortable with the way you attach the microphone to your clothes or hold it in your hand, as well as the places you can use it in the room without generating audio feedback. For hybrid events, test equipment to ensure both online and in-person listeners can hear easily.

Pitch

To enhance your vocal presence, start with grounding your voice, or speaking in a pitch at the low end of your natural range. There are a few reasons for this. First, most speakers' pitch naturally goes up with nervousness. Starting at the lower range can serve as a reminder to yourself to remain relaxed and, if you do get nervous, your voice won't go so high as to strain your vocal cords.

If you are presenting in a virtual or hybrid environment, grounding your pitch will improve the quality of your voice in technology-mediated situations because "everything from microphones to modes of transmission have been optimized for lower voices."[2]

Pitch variety has been found to be the most significant vocal feature that impacts perceived character, competence, sociability, and persuasion.[3] It is important to note that pitch variety does not mean that you need to sound like a stand-up comic or a Shakespearean actor. Enthusiastic speakers need to find places to reign it in. Subdued speakers need to find places to ramp it up. Look for places in your presentation where a change of tone complements the content.

To combat vocal fatigue and technology bias, stand or sit tall with your chest high and shoulders relaxed, tuck your chin to your chest, take a deep breath, and when you exhale, speak in a pitch that is lower than you normally use. Continue lowering your voice until you can no longer make your voice louder; at some point you will lose the ability to project. The lowest part of your authentic vocal range is where you are as low as you can go while still having the ability to project louder than a conversational volume.

Initially, speaking at the low end of your range can feel uncomfortable. Rest assured that it only feels awkward to you because it is a lower pitch than you are in the habit of using. It will sound commanding to your listeners. Work to tap into your grounded voice in presentations, meetings, phone calls, and conversations until it becomes more comfortable.

> *Initially, speaking at the low end of your range can feel uncomfortable.*

While you cannot change your voice to sound like Dennis Haysbert, the actor and spokesperson for Allstate Insurance, you certainly can train yourself to speak at the low end of your natural range to reap the benefits of a lower pitched voice.

Rate

Next, work on speaking slowly and clearly. For most Standard American English speakers, that rate is around 150 words per minute, but this can vary based on the speaker's culture, region, and language background. When presenters get nervous, and most public speakers do, they tend to talk at a fast clip. Dom Barnard did an analysis of nine popular talks on the TED website. He found that the average rate of these speakers was 163 words per minute.[4]

You can compare your rate of speech by watching a recording of your presentation and counting the number of words you say during the course of one minute. Keep in mind that the faster you go, the harder it is for listeners to keep up with our thoughts and the easier it is for you to use junk words (such as "um," "ah," "like," and "so").

Remember to speak more slowly than you think you should. You can do this by crisply articulating every sound, which makes it nearly impossible to rush. And then pause between sentences, which prevents thoughts from running into each other and speeches from getting faster and faster as they progress.

AVOID "SAMESPEAK"

Repeating the same vocal pattern, particularly when that pattern might not "fit" the situation, can cause your audience to lose focus. Having non-stop enthusiasm or monotone can numb an audience to your message. Similarly, "upspeak," or high rising intonation at the end of declarative statements (and not just questions), is often interpreted as lacking in credibility or professionalism. It is important to be aware that upspeak may be a cultural norm. If you visit Australia, upspeak is part of their cadence. Awareness of your sound, and the sound of others, allows you to adapt in ways that will improve your connection to the audience.

Variations

Speaking loudly, lowly, slowly, and clearly is a good start, but not the entire story when it comes to using your voice to its full potential. Just think of the iconic example of Ben Stein playing the boring economics teacher in the 80's film *Ferris Bueller's Day Off*. His painfully monotone voice would call out, "Bueller . . . Bueller . . ." when he was taking roll.

When presenting, take care to vary your tone by emphasizing certain words and inflecting your voice to infuse your words with those "shades of deeper meaning." Take for example the statement:

<u>Madison</u> <u>didn't</u> <u>drive</u> <u>their</u> <u>car</u> into the <u>house</u>.

If you read this sentence five times, each time emphasizing a different underlined portion, you can radically alter the meaning of the sentence. For instance, to emphasize Madison in this sentence suggests that someone other than Madison drove their car into the house.

It is unlikely that you will be discussing driving cars into houses. However, you will be delivering messages to audiences and attempting to convey specific meanings. The use of your voice to highlight those meanings will make you a more effective communicator.

To make the most of your voice as a speaker and to infuse your words with meaning, focus on volume, rate, and pitch. Once you master these basics, then you can turn your focus to vocal variety.

If variety is the spice of life, then vocal variety truly is the spice of speeches. Consider increasing your volume when you repeat a key word or phrase in your speech. The increase in volume, along with the repetition, will make the word or phrase stand out to listeners. Also use a loud whisper to get the attention of your audience. When this technique is used during storytelling, it lends drama and adds suspense to your message.

In terms of rate, you can increase your speed as you reach the climax of a story, then pause, and tell the resolution of the situation in an especially slow, controlled pace. In terms of pitch, you can increase the range of high and low tones in your speaking. This is easiest to do when telling stories and either going into the voices of characters or recreating sounds (for example, the screech of your fender as it rubbed the metal pole in your parking garage).

When it is finally time to deliver your presentation, it is important to warmup your voice. This is even more important if you are working remotely and not speaking with people, even in a casual manner. Check out the vocal warm-up exercises from chapter 2 for some ways to prepare. Effective sound is crucial to the success of any presentation. That importance is heightened in phone calls and virtual presentations with only audio and no video. Ensure you have quality audio equipment that is set up properly. Then focus on tapping into the low, loud, slow, clear, and varied version of your authentic voice.

SPEAKING SPEED BUMPS

Do you talk too fast? Raleen Miller, a speech language pathologist in Washington, D.C., coined four Speaking Speed Bumps to help speakers slow down their rate and improve their intelligibility to listeners. Use these "speaking speed bumps" to slow down.

1. **Drop Your Jaw (DYJ)** Open your mouth wider and move your jaw/chin downward.

   - Do this for words containing short "a" as in at, Adam, band, banana, value, fan, fast, gas, man, snap, capital, panda, package, pants; and

   - Do this for words containing short "o" as in: October, lock, stock, rock, Robert, rocket, dominoes, dock, taco, oxygen, cot, lot;

   - Do this for words containing the "aw" sound as in law, auto, sausage, saw, gone, August, yawn, all, always.

2. **Stretch Your Vowels (SYV)** Do this for words that contain long "e" in the initial, medial, or final position. Retract your lips further back than usual and sustain the long "e" sound. That means you should smile more when saying words such as: me, he, she, either, coffee, even, eat, east, piece, neat, lead, see, seat, mean, and leader.

3. **Two Lips Together (TLT)** During a speech or in daily conversation, whenever you pause, make it a habit to put your two lips together. You should actually feel your lips touching each other. This one movement will significantly diminish your speech rate.

You might be wondering, "When should I pause?" Here are a few suggestions:

   - After a phrase, within a lengthy sentence;

   - Between sentences;

   - Right after you greet someone, before you begin the actual conversation, such as, "Hello, Mike" (TLT) or, "Good afternoon, Senator" (TLT);

   - After responding to a question where the first word you speak is "yes" or "no" and you follow with further comment. For example, somebody at work asks if you have voted today. You answer by saying, "No, (TLT) I'm going to vote on my way home from work."

4. **Punch Your Final Consonants (PYFC)** Emphasize the following final consonant sounds: p, b, d, t, k, g. By doing this, you will slow your rate and people will better understand the words you are speaking. Examples of some words for which you can do this include: that, but, don't, could, help, good, up, lead, lack, mood, head, speak, hired, look, world, had, called, about, hard, right, left, it, important, difficult, can't, bag, and big.

APPLICATION

Review a recent recording of yours (or do a new recording) delivering a virtual presentation or participating in a virtual meeting. Listen to the sound only; you can do this by playing back the audio file, by shutting your eyes, or by covering your image with another window on your computer. How easy is it to understand you? Are you speaking too slowly or too quickly? How expressive are you? How enthusiastic are you? How would you rate the overall sound quality? What could you do with your technology, physical setup, and/or speaking style to improve your sound?

Notes:

1. Sue Shellenbarger, "'Is This How You Really Talk?': Your Voice Affects Others' Perceptions; Silencing the Screeech in the Next Cubicle," *Wall Street Journal*, updated April 23, 2013, https://on.wsj.com/3QxTkao

2. Tina Tallon, "A Century of 'Shrill': How Bias in Technology Has Hurt Women's Voices," *The New Yorker*, September 3, 2019. Accessed April 27, 2022. https://bit.ly/3QSqTuu

3. Judee K. Burgoon, Thomas Birk, and Micael Pfau, "Nonverbal Behaviors, Persuasion, and Credibility," *Human Communication Research* 17, no. 1 (1990): 154.

4. Dom Barnard, "Average Speaking Rate and Words per Minute," *Virtual Speech*, last modified January 20, 2019. https://virtualspeech.com/blog/average-speaking-rate-words-per-minute

Chapter 13

SMILE

An authentic smile is wonderful. A forced smile does not help, and might hurt how an audience perceives a presenter.

That said, we need to come clean—you do not always need to smile during presentations. There are some moments in which a smile would be inappropriate, such as delivering bad news or conveying critical, high stakes information. Additionally, the term "smile" can be fraught. For example, one study found that 98 percent of women respondents have been told to smile at work.[1] Many of those women reported feeling disempowered by this request. Or consider individuals with autism spectrum disorder for whom smiling does not carry the same social cues.[2] Smiling is even associated with racist stereotypes and tropes.[3]

We use the term "smile" to stand for a wide array of facial expressions that are generally meaningful in presenting. One line of research in organizational communication tells us that, for the most part, we are evaluating two traits in the expressions of fellow professionals: competence (i.e., intelligence, power, efficacy, and skill), and warmth (i.e., friendliness, trustworthiness, empathy, and kindness).[4]

As presenters, it is vital to understand what information the audience is receiving about us. Facial expression is part of conveying that. Much like we said about your voice in chapter 12 on sound, we are not asking you to change your face. Some people tend to be very expressive. Others tend to be less expressive. In different situations, each of these might be a virtue. In situations where your default settings might not match how you want to communicate your message, you should have strategies for how to address that mismatch.

It is also worth noting that, as listeners, it is important to not jump to conclusions based on expressiveness. It is one of many inputs. Yes, we naturally assess a scowling person as angry, but with only one datum point, how do we know? We should use this information and seek more to determine our judgment.

The Value of an Authentic Smile

Speakers should strive to engage in a soft smile throughout their presentations and meetings whether they are in person or virtual. Doing so conveys confidence and gives the audience the impression that a presenter is comfortable, even if they feel quite nervous Dr. Brené Brown's 2010 TEDxHouston and 2012 TED Talk are prime examples of effective smiling during presentations.

Smiling also helps build rapport with the audience because it makes the speaker appear friendly, likeable, and approachable. The stronger the connection a speaker builds with his or her listeners, which is particularly important and difficult to do in technology-mediated situations, the more likely the audience will pay attention and respond favorably to the message.

Smiling during a presentation sounds easy enough, but can be hard to remember when nerves kick in. Here are a few crucial times to smile:

Before   *After*

Spoken with Authority Coach Lisa Richard without and with a smile.

Photos courtesy of Lisa Richard.

Before You Say a Word

When you stand at the lectern, stand up in the meeting room, or take control of a virtual meeting, what do you want to convey with your face? In many cases, smiling should be the go-to expression. Hold that smile for a few seconds as you make eye contact with audience members. Take a deep breath and then say the first word of your presentation. Starting with a smile will set the tone of your presentation, help calm your nerves, and increase the chances you will smile throughout the entire speech.

When You Are Struggling

Whether you are struggling with the videoconference technology or finding your place in your notes, smile when things are not going as planned in your speech. Most speakers will give visual cues (grimacing) or auditory fillers (a prolonged "ummmmm") that indicate frustration. Rather than pointing out to your audience that there is a hiccup in your presentation, put on a genuine smile (not a sheepish one), stay silent, and continue when you are ready. By smiling during these uncomfortable moments in your speech, your audience might not even notice you were thrown off.

At the End of Your Speech

You just said the last word of your presentation. Assuming warmth is an appropriate trait to express for the presentation, it is time to look at the audience or your webcam again and smile. This will also cue the emcee, facilitator, or next speaker to take over.

When You Are Listening

There are many times when we are still expressing warmth or competence when not speaking. Whether you are in the audience, on a videoconference, or on a panel but not speaking at the moment, others may still be seeing you. Particularly if you are in a leadership role, on a panel, or in a high-stakes situation, your presentation does not stop when you are done speaking.

Smiling before you start speaking, when you have a hiccup in your speech, at the conclusion of your speech, and while you are listening will certainly help you develop the habit of sharing a smile to connect with your audience. You should also make an effort of smiling throughout your entire presentation. Remind yourself to smile by writing the word "smile" on your outline or by drawing a smiley face on a sticky note and affixing it somewhere near your computer camera where only you can see it. Every time you look into the camera lens, you will be reminded to smile.

The simple act of smiling may be the fastest way to make the greatest improvement in a speech, but it takes time to get into the habit of smiling throughout a presentation. Commit yourself to smiling when you speak, even if you are feeling nervous. Soon enough, you will find that when you are wearing a smile, you will feel as confident on the inside as you look on the outside.

Notes:

1. Marcel Swantes, "A New Study Reveals That Telling Women They Need to Smile Is Bad for Business. Here's Why," *Inc.*, accessed March 31, 2022, https://bit.ly/3A6BS63

2. Eric Patton, "Autism, Attributions and Accommodations: Overcoming Barriers and Integrating a Neurodiverse Workforce," *Personnel Review* 48, no. 4 (2019): 915-34.

3. "Popular and Pervasive Stereotypes of African Americans," *Smithsonian National Museum of African American History & Culture*, October 23, 2018, https://s.si.edu/3QEQe4v

4. Amy J.C. Cuddy, Peter Glick, and Anna Beninger, "The Dynamics of Warmth and Competence Judgments, and Their Outcomes in Organizations," *Research in Organizational Behavior* 31 (2011): 73-98.

Chapter 14

SILENCE

Silence is a powerful tool for speakers—both in terms of avoiding filler words and adding dramatic pauses. Like any tool, the misuse of silence creates problems. For example, a sustained pause in a virtual presentation can cause confusion and even panic that the audio cut out. More often, it is the opposite that is the problem. A speaker fills silences with filler words—also referred to as "junk words" or "discourse markers"—instead of pausing.

Some common junk words and phrases are "like," "so," "you know," and "kind of." Some junk words aren't even words, like "umm" and "uhhh." But speakers can use almost any word, phrase, or sound to intrude in the flow of the presentation, such as "specifically," "precisely," "now," "literally," and even lip-smacking.

Our approach to filler words is guided by two beliefs. One is that the overuse of filler words can create distractions for an audience, lowering engagement with your content and decreasing their estimation of you as a speaker. This is not controversial.

Our second belief is that you don't need to agonize over eliminating every single filler word to the detriment of other areas of delivery or your overall confidence. We've seen speakers catch themselves using a junk word, then go into a tailspin because the presentation is no longer "perfect." That's not good for the speaker or the audience. The presence of a single "umm" will not doom your presentation. It will likely go unnoticed.

> *You don't need to agonize over eliminating every single filler word to the detriment of other areas of delivery or your overall confidence.*

We will focus on the former belief for most of the chapter, but it is worth reducing some of the anxiety over filler words first.

Fillers Exist

In conversation, one in every sixty words that is spoken is a filler word. These words serve cognitive and interactional purposes. Cognitively, fillers in conversation allow for the processing of information. Interactionally, filler words can show politeness or indicate one's intent to respond.[1] Fillers exist and have a function.

That said, presentations are different than conversations. The preparation is different. The length of time we speak is different. The audience size is different. Our expectations are different.

When people say that they want a conversational presentation, what they really mean is that they want the most polished version of the speaker's authentic self. They want the person to be relaxed and confident. They do not mean that they want improvised thoughts, unpracticed delivery, and short contributions that mark speaking in conversation.

The point here is that fillers are not universally bad. If an occasional filler word sneaks into your speech delivery, do not admit defeat and break down. One or two per minute generally go unnoticed and can even be used purposefully in this context, such as communicating an approximation or transitioning to a sensitive topic.

However, extemporaneous and off-the-cuff speakers often use verbal crutches to excess when they are transitioning from one idea to the next because they are not relying on a script. Presenting online often makes matters worse. With the added stresses of navigating a video-conference platform while speaking and the inability to read the nonverbal cues of listeners, many presenters become more addled in technology-mediated situations and their use of filler words skyrockets.

The repetition of filler words and phrases makes speakers appear less polished and can even distract listeners. When used to excess—in the range of ten or more per minute—junk words can undermine a speaker's credibility. You never want listeners to discount the content of your message because it was delivered with a sizeable quantity of junk words.

The solution isn't to do away with your Sandwich Structure Outline (see chapter 5) and switch to a manuscript or memorized speech. Word-for-word scripts almost always lack the conversational tone and authentic quality that listeners crave (and generally require a talented speechwriter and significant rehearsal time to achieve).

> *You never want listeners to discount the content of your message because it is delivered with a sizeable quantity of junk words.*

How, then, can professionals trash the junk words? The purpose of the rest of this chapter is to discuss strategies for reducing filler words in order to allow your best self and your outstanding content to come through.

Identify Junk Words and When You Use Them

The first step is to train yourself to pause briefly rather than using a junk word and to develop awareness of which ones you use and when you use them. To get started, carefully listen to a recent recording of you speaking. Count the number and type of junk words you used. Pay attention to when you use them. Most speakers start sentences with them; turn sentences in to long run-on sentences with them; insert them where there should be a comma; or fill time with junk words when they are looking at notes, formulating what to say next, or fiddling with videoconference technology.

Soon, you will become aware of your use of junk words in real time, during presentations, and in everyday conversations. While annoying, this knowledge is crucial—if you can't hear junk words in a routine meeting, it isn't likely you will hear and avoid them during a high-stakes client pitch or job interview.

Practice Putting Your Lips Together

Next, focus on putting your lips together in silence instead of using junk words. When your lips are together, you cannot utter a junk word, phrase, or sound. One way to develop this habit is to use our Hand Clap, Toe Tap Method of rehearsing. To use this method, do two rehearsals to learn content and make final refinements to your outline. During the next two rehearsals, clap your hands and press your lips together each time you get to a period or comma in your speaking. The sound of the hand clap makes it less awkward to pause because there is still sound and no silence.

For your fifth and sixth rehearsals, tap your toe on the ground and put your lips together when you get to a pausing place. The sound of the toe tap will be softer than a hand clap, but still audible. For your final rehearsals with technology and the actual virtual presentation, do an inaudible toe tap (if sitting) or grip your toes in your shoes (if standing) while you put your lips together and pause in silence. The Hand Clap, Toe Tap Method works because you are replacing one habit (using junk words) with another less problematic habit (pausing and doing a physical movement). Replacing one habit with another, like chewing gum for smoking, is an easier way to change an engrained habit. The more fluent you are with your content and technology, the more bandwidth your brain has to focus on silence and avoiding junk words. (See chapter 17 for more on rehearsals.)

Beware of Long Pauses in Virtual and Hybrid Contexts

In live presentations, a long pause can make a story more exciting or emphasize a crucial point. Extended silence can even be a powerful rhetorical strategy—just watch the speech delivered on March 24, 2018, at the March for Our Lives in Washington, DC, by X Gonzales, a survivor of the Marjory Stoneman Douglas High School mass shooting in Parkland, FL.

Unlike in-person speakers, virtual presenters have to be cautious with long pauses. After all, audience members may be confused by the silence because they might think there is a glitch or delay in the technology. To prevent confusion, speakers using computer-mediated communication should announce pauses longer than a few seconds and give verbal directions on what listeners should be doing during the pause. The speaker may even reinforce the verbal with written instructions, such as on a slide or in the chat box of the videoconference platform.

If you use a long pause in a virtual meeting, other participants might miss nonverbal cues that you intend to continue speaking and could cut you off. To prevent interruptions, prepare key points in advance and enumerate them ("there are three reasons why I support this recommendation"). If someone does interrupt, you can more easily regain the floor ("I promised three reasons, let me share the third before we move on").

When you facilitate virtual meetings, you can manage pauses, so they don't become problematic. For example, you can ask a meeting participant who paused if they were truly done sharing their thoughts ("Thanks for that perspective. Did you have anything else to add?"). If you want to get perspectives from attendees, announce the speaking order. If you do not anticipate the effect of pauses, you will have a situation similar to a four-way stop when several cars arrive at the same time and no-one knows who should go. Your preview of speakers will make transitions faster, smoother, and less awkward. Plus, you can increase inclusion by calling on meeting participants who don't normally unmute themselves to chime in.

Similarly, in hybrid situations, speakers need to remember that audience members are encountering the presentation in two vastly different modes. In the room, the audience members might see that a speaker is scrolling on their computer to find an answer or that a question was asked away from a microphone. Those online might not see or hear in the same way. Or a question might be asked in the chat box and the speaker is preparing to answer, but in-room attendees might not be aware. In those cases, it is helpful for the speaker to explain the pauses to keep all in the audience apprised of what's happening.

Using the occasional filler word can have a purpose and shouldn't derail a presentation. Overall, speakers should focus on reducing junk words and replacing them with silence to sound crisp and confident. Experienced educators, presenters, and meeting facilitators should strive to use purposeful and dramatic pauses to elevate their speaking.

HOW MANY JUNK WORDS IS TOO MANY?

It is perfectly appropriate to use zero, one, or two junk words per minute of speaking. Sporadic use of junk words is conversational and can even be done purposefully to hold the floor during a meeting or conversation to prevent interruptions. If you use an average of three, four, or five junk words per minute, listeners will not be consciously aware of your use of them. They may, however, make subconscious and negative judgments about your competence and confidence based on this use. When you use six to ten junk words per minute, listeners will become aware of them and may find it difficult to focus on your message. If you use more than ten junk words per minute, you are in the danger zone. Your listeners will be distracted, and you will undermine your credibility.

APPLICATION

1. Calculate your average filler word-per-minute rate by carefully counting each filler word you hear when playing back a two- to five-minute clip of a recently recorded presentation (or a rehearsal of an upcoming presentation). Divide the number of junk words into the number of minutes. For example, if you heard 20 junk words in 2 minutes and 30 seconds, you would calculate: 20 junk words, divided by 2.5 minutes, equals 8 junk words per minute. Another way to estimate your junk words-per-minute rate is using the Presenter Coach tool in newer versions of Microsoft PowerPoint. After you calculate your baseline use of junk words, complete the Hand Clap, Toe Tap Method for rehearsing as explained in this chapter. Calculate your junk word per minute rate again after your final technical dress rehearsal or actual presentation to measure your progress.

2. Listen carefully during an upcoming meeting. Tally the number of junk words each participant uses during their speaking role(s). How did the number of junk words influence your ability to follow the speaker's message? How did they impact your perception of each speaker's level of confidence, professionalism, and polish? How did the specific junk words used ("um" versus "like" for example) impact your perceptions of the speaker? How can you apply your observations to your own speaking and use of filler words?

Notes:

1. Saumya Kalia, "Science Backs People Who Use Filler Words Like 'Um' and 'You Know,'" *The Swaddle*, August 21, 2021, accessed April 15, 2022, https://theswaddle.com/filler-words-um-you-know/.

Chapter 15

SIGHT

Making eye contact with members of your audience is key to conveying confidence and establishing rapport. Sight is one of the most difficult skills to transition from in-person communication to virtual and hybrid communication. This chapter will explore strategies to enhance your eye contact for online, in-person, and hybrid speaking situations.

> *Sight is one of the most difficult skills to transition from in-person communication to virtual and hybrid communication.*

Look Up From Your Materials

Think back to a speech when the presenter was reading a script with their nose buried in the text. It can be painful or just boring. Presenting from a manuscript is difficult to do well; it not only requires expertly written material to achieve an engaging tone, but it also requires copious rehearsals and ideally a teleprompter to simulate eye contact with audience members. Even then, eye contact from manuscript delivery can be difficult to achieve.

Most speakers aren't trained speechwriters, don't have the time to commit to practice reading a script until it reads naturally, and don't have a teleprompter. That is why most presenters should use the extemporaneous mode—speaking from a well-researched and rehearsed outline—so they can look at people in their audience and talk to them conversationally, rather than read to them. It is acceptable to glance at your notes regularly as the goal is not to memorize your remarks. Practice will help make references to notes brief. Aim to pause in silence when glancing down and speak to listeners while looking up. (See chapter 17 for more on effective rehearsals.)

For the majority of speakers, the first step toward making meaningful eye contact is using and rehearsing an outline consisting of words and phrases rather than reading a word-for-word script or using PowerPoint slides filled with text. This format forces presenters to speak conversationally and frees their eyes to look up from notes. Such an approach is transferable across presentation modes, be it in person, virtual, or hybrid. (See chapter 5 on outlining presentations with the Sandwich Structure and chapter 9 on presentation aids.)

Make Lasting Eye Contact

After the eyes are freed to look up, speakers must then make lasting eye contact. How one achieves this can differ depending on the presentation mode.

In Person

When speaking in person, scanning the room without maintaining direct eye contact with any audience member will not cut it. It is also important to avoid focusing on something other than the audience (e.g., glancing out a window, up at the ceiling, or down at the floor). You do not want to focus your gaze on the wall in the back of the room looking above the heads of your listeners. This behavior will seem strange to audience members and they might actually look behind them to see what it is that you are looking at.

Instead, look directly at someone in the audience while saying a sentence or making one complete point—three full seconds of unbroken eye contact is ideal. (Note that unbroken eye contact means no blinking or glances up or down.) Rest assured that three seconds of unbroken eye contact is not a stare down; it is a sign of a confident speaker who is connecting with listeners. (Note that eye contact norms do vary among cultures, so research appropriate and respectful levels of eye contact ahead of time when engaging in intercultural communication.)

Aim to make lasting eye contact with as many people as you can. For large audiences, don't look at the same few people repeatedly or focus only on people who are nodding and smiling. Make lasting eye contact with a random selection of people in different parts of the audience.

> *Aim to make lasting eye contact with as many audience members as you can. For large audiences, make lasting eye contact with a random selection of people.*

Lasting eye contact might feel awkward to some presenters, particularly ones who are neuro-divergent or who are not in the habit of making lasting eye contact in everyday conversations. Such speakers can practice by gazing at the tip of the nose or between the eyes of listeners and gradually increasing the amount of time they lock their gaze with eyes of listeners in informal speaking situations. This will lay the groundwork for enhancing eye contact in one-on-one, small group, and even public-speaking situations.

Virtual

Neurotypical humans are hardwired to use eye contact to connect with other humans.[1] That's why it is extremely difficult to hold your gaze with a piece of camera equipment and not at the screen (where the virtual connection would seem to occur). However, that is what you need to do to give virtual listeners the most robust experience of eye contact from you. If you only look at their images on your computer screen (as is natural), audience members will

| *Before* | *After* |

Spoken with Authority Coach Lynne Adrine looking down and looking directly into the camera.

Photos courtesy of Lynne Adrine.

see the top of your head and it will look as if you are reading your notes instead of speaking confidently.

Eye contact is vital, yet its effectiveness is diluted online. As a result, you should aim to make eye contact with the camera for about 80-90 percent of your presenting time. Do not worry about "staring down" online listeners. Long and unbroken stretches of eye contact in computer-mediated situations does not make listers uncomfortable as it would in face-to-face speaking situations.

You can significantly improve eye contact by arranging the gallery of virtual listeners on your computer screen right below your camera lens. By looking at images of audience members near your camera, you can improve the experience of eye contact without fully staring into the lens. This is less awkward and a good place to start for many speakers. As you gain experience with virtual speaking, aim to look directly into the lens of your camera. The most effective way to do this is to eliminate the listener gallery (an option on most videoconference platforms), because you will have no faces to distract you from the camera lens. Another strategy is to tape a small picture of a loved one right above or next to the camera lens to draw your eye up to the camera lens.

Keep your outline or notes as close to the camera lens as possible instead of on the table or desk where you are presenting. The goal is to keep your chin up so listeners never see the top of your head. Two ways to place notes closer to the camera lens are: (1) Tape your outline to the wall, a large cardboard box, or a lamp that you can position right behind your computer. Position your notes just above the computer screen so your eyes don't have to stray far from the camera lens to locate your next discussion point; and (2) Create a "peacock" of Post-It Notes around your laptop screen or computer monitor out of sight of your camera lens and not covering it. Each sticky note will have a reminder of your next key idea. Start on the bottom left; work across the top of your computer screen; then, go down the right side. Even if you have a second computer monitor, use paper notes to prevent a technology failure that leaves you without your talking points during an online presentation or meeting.

Hybrid

In a hybrid environment, it is quite easy to lose track of either the in-person or online audience. Or, in being attentive to both audiences, you might feel like your head is spinning when trying to connect with each one.

The good news is that eye contact is not a competition. It is not a race to see how fast you can look at everyone. If we treated it this way, then we would lose the "meaningful" part of eye contact and it would be absolutely nerve-wracking.

In the hybrid setting, approach eye contact with intent. Consider selecting portions where you will focus on just the in-person audience, then another portion during which you will present to the virtual group. Be sure to look into the camera whenever directly addressing online attendees or responding to a question from a remote participant. If you feel comfortable connecting with each audience, you can deviate from your plan and make eye contact based on instinct. Starting with clear intentions and a plan will put you and your audience at ease.

Coordinate Body Position with Gaze

Once you are making lasting eye contact, increase your connection with listeners by turning your head and body to face the person you are looking at (as opposed to keeping your head and body positioned straight ahead and looking out of the corner of your eye). Also, remember to keep your chin tucked; nobody in your audience wants you to look down your nose at them. Then, repeat this sustained, quality eye contact with another person in the audience in another part of the room.

To enhance sight in virtual presentations, make sure your camera lens is at eye level because looking up or down at it will diminish the experience listeners have of receiving eye contact from you. If your laptop is on a desk or your lap, you will be looking down at the camera. Set it on a few thick books or on a sturdy box on a table or desk to get it to the correct level. If you have a desktop computer, the camera may be too high, so you may need to lower it or raise your chair to achieve eye level.

Coordinating your stance and sight in hybrid presentations might take some forethought. Moving within the room might enhance your eye contact for one audience, but it might take you out of frame for the other. Similarly, how you position yourself to engage with the online attendees might block you from the others in the room. There might not be a perfect solution. The key is to diagnose the situation before the presentation starts and to develop a plan. Your composure will go a long way in signaling to the audience that you have everything under control.

Making lasting eye contact is crucial for demonstrating your confidence as a presenter as well as establishing a connection with listeners. Effectively maintaining your gaze with audience members requires practice. Practice getting comfortable holding eye contact as well as with the content of the presentation so you don't have to constantly refer to your notes.

APPLICATION

1. Enlist the help of a friend or family member (in person, if possible). Make sustained eye contact with your partner for three full seconds while counting aloud, "One Mississippi, two Mississippi, three Mississippi." How did it feel to engage in eye contact for this length of time? Did you have the impulse to blink or glance away before three seconds was up? What can you do to maintain eye contact more effectively with people you are speaking to and to hold your gaze even longer on the camera lens during computer-mediated communication?

2. Practice a two- to three-minute recording of an upcoming or recent presentation and record it in a videoconference platform. Change the placement of your laptop. Put it on your lap and record, and then put the computer on a table. Lastly put the computer on a small box or steady stack of books. What do you notice about the angle? Which one allows you to make the most effective eye contact? Once you identify the best angle for your computer (hint: it's not on your lap), experiment with where you put your speaking notes. Try laying the printed notes on your desk or table and recording your presentation. Then try recording having the notes on your keyboard. Also try putting your notes on a higher level by taping them above your computer screen to a lamp, box, or wall. Notice how your ability to make effective eye contact in online contexts is impacted by the placement of your computer and speaking notes.

Notes:

1. Melinda Wenner Moyer, "Eye Contact: How Long Is Too Long?" *Scientific American*, January 1, 2016. www.scientificamerican.com/article/eye-contact-how-long-is-too-long

Chapter 16

SETUP

Before the pandemic, technology and speaking space was largely dictated to professional speakers. Your organization assigned you a desk and computer in the office. It had conference rooms where meetings were held. Event organizers booked a hotel or event venue to host larger crowds. But times have changed.

According to an analysis of data by the career-site Ladders, only 4 percent of high-paying jobs were remote before the pandemic.[1] The same study found the number of remote positions increased to 9 percent by the end of 2020, 18 percent by the end of 2021, and projected that this trend will continue increasing despite a reduction in pandemic-related restrictions. Pointing to the same trends of more remote work and computer-mediated communication, a survey conducted by FlexJobs found that "58 percent [of respondents] said they want a fully remote job, while 39 percent prefer a hybrid arrangement. Only 3 percent want to return to fully in-person work."[2]

It is clear that computer-mediated communication will forever be a part of the business landscape. Even for professionals who work fully in person, there is a good chance that they are regularly logging in to videoconference platforms from their office for virtual meetings and other events. For professionals who haven't already invested in their online presence, it is time to optimize their videoconference platform, computer, internet, and AV equipment to enhance platform performance, productivity, and professionalism in virtual meetings. This chapter is dedicated to how this can be accomplished and will provide tips for enhancing setup for face-to-face communication situations as well.

Videoconference Platform

Get comfortable with the videoconference platform that will be used for your speaking role. While you have become proficient with a platform or two that you use most frequently, it can be unsettling to switch. Also, when reaching out to clients, prospective clients, or others you invite to attend a virtual meeting or presentation, do some audience analysis and adaptation by finding out what platform is most convenient for them, offering to use it, and working out the technology on your end ahead of time. You don't want to waste valuable and limited meeting time sorting out IT issues.

Do make sure that you optimize the videoconference platform. Regularly update its software and enable functions like live captioning (a transcription service that makes virtual experiences more inclusive for people who are hard of hearing or who speak a different language).

For virtual meetings and events that have large or public audiences, prevent so-called "Zoom-bombing" by sharing the meeting link privately, using a password, and disabling videoconference functions for participants. Also, have a co-host or producer to help monitor for inappropriate uses of the chat box, screen share, and other videoconference features, and practice how to remove a malevolent meeting attendee from your virtual event. Consider drafting an email to participants with back-up meeting information should you need to end a virtual event and pivot quickly due to an internet troll or technical glitch.

Computer

After you update software and lock down the security features on your videoconference platform, focus on how to optimize it by making some adjustments on your computer. To help prevent freezes, delays, or blurring on your videoconference platform, quit any unnecessary applications on your computer that are using up memory and processing power. On Windows, hold down Control+Shift+Esc to open Task Manager. On a Mac, close any apps that have a black dot under them in your dashboard or open the Activity Monitor app in Utilities. Also, if you haven't restarted your computer lately, take time to update your operating system and software before your technical dress rehearsal—you do not want to make changes to your computer that will impact the settings or functioning of the videoconference platform after you rehearsed with them.

Using an Ethernet cable to connect your computer directly to your router or Internet access point will make the connection faster and more reliable. If hardwiring your computer is not an option, sitting close to your router or using a Wi-Fi signal booster can reduce choppy video and delayed audio. If at all possible, reduce competition for bandwidth by asking housemates if they would delay nonessential uses of the internet. Finally, don't forget to plug in your power cord; videoconferencing can quickly drain your computer battery.

Audio

While your computer's built-in camera is generally sufficient for video, computer audio is a different story. At the very least, use an inexpensive earbud-microphone combination that will get the microphone closer to your mouth and away from the sounds of typing and your computer's fan. Opt for a wired headset to prevent delays or distortions that can occur with Bluetooth-enabled devices. If you spend several hours each week leading virtual meetings, speaking on phone or videoconference calls, delivering online speeches, conducting webinars, or podcasting, it makes sense to upgrade to a high-quality microphone with a pop filter (to prevent a popping sound when you start or end words with the letters P or B).

> *While your computer's built-in camera is generally sufficient for video, computer audio is a different story.*

Check the settings of your videoconference platform and select your add-on speaker (output) and microphone (input) instead of the built-in audio. Speaking of audio settings and etiquette, make sure to mute your audio when you enter a meeting and only unmute when speaking. Reducing background noises from each virtual meeting attendee will greatly enhance the sound quality for everyone. Also, turn off your computer and phone notifications to prevent the distracting dinging sound each time you receive an email or text message. Please, never eat or drink on microphone—it amplifies and makes intolerable chewing and gulping sounds.

Visual

Most computers and laptops have a decent camera. If your built-in camera will suffice, make sure you remove anything covering the camera and clean the lens. Use a stack of books or a computer stand to ensure it is positioned properly at eye level.

If your computer camera is subpar or located low on a laptop or high on a monitor such that it is difficult to position at eye level, get an external camera for virtual meetings. One budget friendly option if you have a newer smartphone is to use an app to turn it into a webcam. Most smartphones have powerful video capability and are up for the task—just make sure you have a tripod to stabilize the lens at eye level for your videoconferences.

If you are an in-person speaker at a hybrid event, you will want to use your smartphone on a tripod at the very least. Consider hiring a videographer with professional-grade AV equipment so the feed to online participants is high quality. Virtual attendees of hybrid events should be able to easily see and hear both the speaker and presentation aids.

When you are participating in a virtual meeting, you can often achieve acceptable lighting from a nearby window. The light source should be in front of you, not from the side or behind, and should not be obstructed (no shades or blinds with slats that will cast distracting shadows). If it is dark outside or if you are often leading meetings or webinars, supplement with a light ring or cube to significantly brighten your appearance. Pay attention to what is highlighted behind you.

Before *After*

Spoken with Authority Coach David Henderson without artificial lighting and with artificial lighting.

Photos courtesy of David Henderson.

Background

Your background on a virtual meeting or webinar is an extension of your clothing. Select your background as you would a tie, necklace, or other accessory. Decide if you want something understated or if you want to make a statement. For the former, sit in front of a plain painted wall. For the latter, you might set up your speaking area in front of a bookcase if you are an avid reader or researcher, a plant or flower if you are a nature lover, or a statement piece of art if you are a creative type. Whatever your approach, be as thoughtful and proactive with your background as you would be with clothing choices for an important meeting or presentation.

> *Your background on a virtual meeting or webinar is an extension of your clothing.*

Make sure to declutter and curate what is in view of the camera so it is simple and not distracting. If you cannot reduce clutter, use the blur feature on your videoconference platform to remove visual distractions behind you. Also, avoid having a door or entryway behind you on camera; this can be the source of unwanted cameos from housemates and pets.

Wear clothes that coordinate with your setting, but that don't blend in. Avoid tight stripes which can jump on camera, and saturated reds which can bleed. Remember to sit close to the camera and frame the camera view so listeners see more than a talking head—chest up is ideal.

Before

After

Spoken with Authority Coach Jean Miller sitting back from and close to the camera..

Photos courtesy of Jean Miller.

If you have a small space, housemates, or the need for more personal privacy, consider using the blur feature or a custom virtual background. Under no circumstance should you use the preloaded options of the Golden Gate Bridge or the Northern Lights for a work meeting or presentation; these are obviously fake and, quite frankly, weird. You can purchase a stock photo of a bookcase or office setting. Your organization may also have images of the office or their logo that you can upload for a custom virtual background.

To create a professional looking custom virtual background (that can also be consistent across speakers in multiple locations), purchase and use green-screen technology. This bright green cloth backdrop is used in movie production as well as the weather report on the news to project a desired background behind the subject. The color contrast enables your computer to superimpose you more effectively on your selected background image, making the resulting image crisper and more professional. Before you dismiss the idea of a green screen, research a few options. They are less expensive than you may think, come in collapsible versions, and can transport easily along with your microphone and computer stand so you can have a professional online presence whether you are speaking virtually from home, from your office building, or even from a travel destination!

Before | *After*

Spoken with Authority Founder Christine Clapp using a preloaded Zoom virtual background with no green screen and a custom uploaded virtual background with a green screen.

Photos courtesy of Christine Clapp.

Remember that your background now serves as an accessory to your clothing, similar to socks, shoes, a handbag, or jewelry. Select clothes that coordinate with your backdrop but choose ones that do not blend in such as a contrasting color. If your background is plain, consider a bold color (not red) or a pattern (not tight stripes) to add visual interest.

Sample setup with a green screen,
artificial lighting, laptop stand,
and external microphone.

Photos courtesy of Christine Clapp.

While set-up requires heightened attention for computer-mediated communication that takes place in a home office or office building, you can enhance the setup for in-person speaking roles too. Here are several tips:

- Test technology for in-person meetings and events. This provides time to troubleshoot issues with the AV and IT systems ensuring the audience has a quality experience. A technical dress rehearsal also gives you experience in the speaking space and using the equipment, reducing your level of stress, and increasing your ability to connect with listeners.

- Use a microphone for any meeting larger than a group that fits around a conference table so everyone can hear. Hearing loss is an invisible disability that impacts 15 percent of American adults.[3]

- Consider where you sit. For meetings, avoid sitting in front of a window. The back lighting can make the edges of your body more diffuse and reduce your physical presence. When possible, sit in front of a solid wall and wear a contrasting color. Your placement at a conference table is also important. If you want to take charge, sit at the head of the table. If your goal is inclusion and collaboration, find a location with a round table. If you want to avoid an adversarial dynamic, sit next to and not across from the person or people who can be oppositional.

- Consider your clothes. To enhance your physical presence, wear a jacket or blazer with structured shoulders. If you are speaking on a stage, be mindful of the setting. Find out what color the backdrop or curtain is. If it is black or blue, avoid wearing mostly black or blue and opt for gray instead. If the stage has a red curtain, your black or blue clothing will contrast well. If you are speaking on a panel of experts, inquire about the seating arrangements. If organizers are seating speakers in overstuffed chairs, on a couch, or at a table with no skirt on the front, consider wearing pants or a long dress to avoid feelings of discomfort or a wardrobe malfunction. It is a smart idea to travel with backup clothes so you have options should you find the backdrop colors or seating arrangement is incompatible with your initial clothing selections . . .or if you happen to spill coffee or mustard on yourself before a speaking role.

- Consider your shoes. Shoes with a heel do make you taller and enhance your physical presence. They make some speakers feel more confident, while they make other speakers feel uncomfortable. Be purposeful about rehearsing in the shoes you intend to wear during your presentation. If you do not feel confident, comfortable, and grounded, do not wear those shoes. Heels and uncomfortable leather shoes are not required. More and more professionals are transitioning to "crossover" footwear that combines the formal look of a dress shoe with the comfortable feel of a sneaker. Others are deciding to make a statement by wearing high-end sneakers in professional settings. No matter what style of shoes makes you feel confident, comfortable, and grounded, your footwear should be squeaky clean and recently polished.

Whether you are in an online, in person, or hybrid speaking role, paying attention and making adjustments to your equipment, setting, and clothing will elevate your effectiveness, confidence, and professionalism as a presenter.

APPLICATION

1. Watch two virtual commencement addresses delivered in May 2020: Former President Barack Obama to HBCU graduates, and fiction author James Patterson for the University of Wisconsin, Madison. How were their backgrounds and clothing appropriate for their intended audience? What could they have done differently to improve on their setting and/or attire?

2. Coco Chanel advised that we remove one accessory before leaving the house. If your backdrop is an extension of your look, what is one element that you could remove or change to improve the experience of your online presentation for viewers and communicate the appropriate tone?

Notes:

1. "Data: Nearly 20percent of All Professional Jobs Are Now Remote," *Ladders*, January 3, 2022, accessed April 29, 2022, https://bit.ly/3AsjTlt

2. Rachel Pelta, "Many Workers Have Quit or Plan to After Employers Revoke Remote Work, *Flexjobs*, accessed April 29, 2022, https://www.flexjobs.com/blog/post/workers-quit-employers-revoke-remote-work/

3. "Quick Statistics about Hearing," *National Institute of Deafness and Other Communication Disorders*, accessed April 29, 2022, https://www.nidcd.nih.gov/health/statistics/quick-statistics-hearing

CHECKLIST FOR PRESENTATION DELIVERY

STANCE

- ☐ Am I standing with feet planted and hip-width apart?
- ☐ Am I sitting close to the camera and using a firm chair for computer-mediated communication?
- ☐ Are my hands at my sides in a neutral position between purposeful and authentic gestures?
- ☐ Are my shoulders back, chest proud, head high, and chin tucked?

SOUND

- ☐ Am I using a quality microphone?
- ☐ Am I projecting loudly?
- ☐ Am I speaking slowly and articulating clearly?
- ☐ Am I adding variations in pitch, rate and tone to add interest?

SMILE

- ☐ Am I speaking with energy and enthusiasm?
- ☐ Am I using facial expressions consistent with my emotional tone?

SILENCE

- ☐ Am I replacing junk words with silence?
- ☐ Am I limiting junk words to two or three per minute?
- ☐ Am I pausing between sentences or am I stringing separate thoughts together?

SIGHT

- ☐ Am I glancing at my notes occasionally and briefly?
- ☐ Am I positioning my notes to improve my eye contact?
- ☐ Am I holding my gaze on the eyes of listeners for three full seconds when in person?
- ☐ Am I holding my gaze on my camera lens 80 to 90 percent of the time when online?

SETUP

- ☐ Am I using a strong Internet connection and up-to-date computer and videoconference platform?
- ☐ Am I optimizing audio by using a wired microphone and turning off notifications?
- ☐ Am I getting my camera to eye level?
- ☐ Am I using artificial lighting to brighten my appearance?
- ☐ Am I curating a professional and uncluttered backdrop or using a custom virtual background and greenscreen?
- ☐ Am I avoiding clothing with saturated reds and tight patterns for computer-mediated communication?

Chapter 17

REHEARSALS

There is one reason why many presenters are anxious, and many presentations are underwhelming: speakers do not rehearse nearly enough. This lack of practice is only exacerbated with virtual and hybrid presentations when speakers must contend with the added stress of managing a videoconference platform and building rapport with remote audience members.

What are the causes of this lack of rehearsal? First, speakers start working on presentations too late. A major speech requires at least a month for adequate rehearsals, an important briefing or pitch should have at least one week for rehearsals, and a routine meeting should have several days for rehearsals. You will want to allocate a longer time for rehearsing if you are new to the type of presentation, if **you are new** to the topic or audience, or new to the videoconference platform or technology for audience engagement.

Second, presenters spend too much of their preparation time perfecting content. While content is key to the success of a presentation, it is not uncommon, especially for speakers who make the mistake of scripting their remarks, to spend 90 percent of preparation time writing and tinkering with their remarks. That's too much. This leaves inadequate time for saying the presentation aloud, becoming familiar and fluid with the material, and making the delivery dynamic.

Third, many speakers simply do not know how to rehearse. How many times should you rehearse?

At least six.

Yes, that's right. You should rehearse a minimum of six times. To remember how many rehearsals, just think, "Six sticks." When you rehearse six times, the material becomes "sticky" in your mind and easier to recall even when you get a jolt of nervous energy before an audience.

You might be thinking, "I'll never have enough time to rehearse that much!" or "I'll sound too stiff and robotic. I'll be more conversational if I just wing it."

Rest assured, our method of rehearsing doesn't take more time overall. It calls on you to craft a detailed outline and to say it aloud much earlier in the process than you would for scripted remarks. Instead of spending 90 percent of time writing content and 10 percent practicing it, aim for 40 percent of time outlining and 60 percent of time practicing your presentation out loud (because you do not gain muscle memory with content when you say it "in your head").

> *Rest assured, our method of rehearsing doesn't take more time overall.*

Our method for rehearsing also contributes to a more confident and conversational delivery of carefully crafted content. It could be true that winging your remarks may lead to a less halting delivery than speaking from a Sandwich Structure Outline with little or no practice. However, winging it comes at the great cost of missing key points you hoped to make or of going on tangents that dilute your message.

As you will learn in the following overview of what to do and expect during each of your six rehearsals, the first few run throughs with a Sandwich Structure Outline are typically rocky— that's to be expected. Even the most celebrated speakers do not have their speech down on a second run through. In fact, the people who make public speaking look the most effortless are those who have practiced their craft and their material the most. So, keep practicing even if it feels hard or awkward.

There is something special about getting to the sixth rehearsal. It typically is the sixth rehearsal when speakers internalize their content, make fewer and briefer glances at their outline, recover quickly from hiccups in their delivery, and feel significantly more confident and present at the lectern. It is the rehearsal at which you free up mental bandwidth from focusing on "What do I say next?" to "How do I say it dynamically?"

Now you know how many rehearsals you require. Following is what you should do and what to expect each time you practice.

Rehearsals 1 and 2:

For these initial practices, speak from a well-researched and carefully crafted Sandwich Structure outline. It is not advisable to start rehearsing before you have completed your research on the audience and situation (see chapter 3), established a concrete messaging strategy (see chapter 4), and developed a working draft of your speech outline (see chapter 5).

Do not wait until your outline is perfect to start rehearsing—you will put it off for too long and you will not have time for all the rehearsals. Start rehearsing when you are 75 to 80 percent ready with your content. Do not worry that it will be an underbaked final presentation; you will make improvements to the content of your speech in your initial rehearsals. Besides, it is better to give a speech where both the content and delivery are at 85 percent ready rather than one where the content is at 100 percent and the delivery is completely unpolished. Remember, it takes at least several days to rehearse for a routine presentation and a month or more for a formal speech.

> *Do not wait until your outline is perfect to start rehearsing— you will put it off for too long and you will not have time for all the rehearsals.*

For your first two rehearsals, speak sitting down in a comfortable spot. Do not worry about your delivery style; focus on the content of the presentation—getting familiar with it and identifying where you need to edit for clarity, flow, and length.

Expect a rocky delivery that comes in fits and starts. You may find it difficult to explain points clearly and concisely, and transitions will be rough. Do not start from the beginning every time you make a mistake. It is important to complete each rehearsal. If you restart every time you make a mistake, you will have a very well-rehearsed introduction and be quite unfamiliar with later parts of the presentation. Get in the habit of continuing your presentation. After all, it is good practice for hiccups that might happen before an audience.

Use a stopwatch to determine whether you have significantly too much or too little material, and proactively edit your presentation. It is never a good idea to ignore time constraints or plan to rush through material to fit it in your allotted time. You may also find in these first rehearsals that you need to edit the arrangement of some points to make the presentation more coherent or to add stories to add color to facts and figures. Do expect to make changes in your early rehearsals. You will be improving content and laying the foundation for effective delivery at the same time.

Rehearsals 3 and 4:

For your next two rehearsals, continue working off the Sandwich Structure Outline you edited after your initial rehearsals. Deliver your presentation from the position you will take for the actual presentation (sitting or standing) and using videoconference platform, slides, audience-engagement tools, and other presentation aids you prepared for the final presentation. Despite the popular advice to practice in front of a mirror, avoid this technique. It can be unnecessarily distracting and trains speakers to focus on themselves rather than their message and audience.

Expect to be more fluent with your material on the third and fourth rehearsals, but don't be surprised when you go blank and can't remember what you wanted to say, or struggle with the wording of ideas or the transitions between points. This is normal. You might make some notations on your outline during these rehearsals, but avoid making major changes to the content or to the notes you will speak from (as you will develop a memory of where things are on your outline so you can find your point easily or remember without looking down).

> *Expect to be more fluent with your material on the third and fourth rehearsals.*

Continue to practice with a stopwatch. You can expect more consistency with the length of the speech and the timing of specific parts, such as the introduction, main points, and conclusion.

Rehearsals 5 and 6:

For the fifth and sixth rehearsals, speak from the outline you are now familiar with. Deliver your speech with the technology setup that closely resembles the speaking situation you will encounter on presentation day.

Expect to feel more comfortable with your speech content. It will come off your tongue much easier at this point. You will start to form patterns in the way you say certain parts of the presentation, though each time you say it will be a little different because it is not scripted or memorized. Now that you are gaining command of your speech content, there will be fewer hiccups in your delivery. And when you do stumble, you will be able to recover much more quickly and gracefully.

Do not get frustrated when your phrasing is awkward or when you start a sentence and wish you constructed it differently. It is more important to have a connection with your listeners than perfection with your message. There is no such thing as a perfect speech, so go with the flow and don't emphasize small mistakes that inevitably happen when speaking conversationally from an outline rather than reading a manuscript. Your audience doesn't know what you planned, so don't clue them in when you deviate.

> *It is more important to have a connection with your listeners than perfection with your message.*

Start to hone your delivery (see chapters 10 to 16 for more detail). Turn your attention to avoiding speaking habits that will distract your audience from your message and focus on making your style more dynamic. This is the point at which analyzing a video recording of your rehearsals is especially useful. As you review a video of you speaking, remember not to be overly critical of yourself. Pretend like you are giving feedback to a close friend or mentee—a person you care about and wouldn't hold to an unrealistic standard.

Keep timing yourself. Your rehearsals should be quite consistent in length without even having to glance at your timer during the run through.

Rehearsal 7+ / Dress Rehearsals:

When you reach practice seven and greater, you have graduated to the dress rehearsal. For these fine-tuning and technology-check sessions, continue to speak from your familiar outline and place it where it will be for the actual presentation. (See chapter 15 for placement of notes to enhance eye contact.) Do not change the format of your outline or make major changes in the content now!

You may not need to refer to your outline often but keep it with you. When you get nervous in your dress rehearsals and especially on presentation day, you will find yourself taking glances at it. There is no shame in having notes and using them; it is undoubtedly better to pause and look down at an outline to get back on track if you lose your train of thought than it is to struggle needlessly and awkwardly during a presentation. Aim to look down at your outline while you pause and look up to speak so it doesn't appear like you are relying on your notes.

It's important to deliver your dress rehearsals with the technology and setup you will be using on speech day whether your presentation is in person, online, or hybrid. Testing, optimizing, and troubleshooting AV and IT equipment is key to reducing anxiety and ensuring your presentation goes smoothly. Event organizers are usually eager to accommodate your request for a dress rehearsal—they appreciate your willingness to invest care in your presentation and the audience experience.

For your dress rehearsals, focus on getting comfortable with the location and setup, as well as conveying enthusiasm in your speech. Think about vocal variations, gestures, facial expressions, and dramatic pauses you can use to make your presentation more interesting and memorable for listeners. Again, recording and reviewing your dress rehearsals will help improve your delivery.

> *It's important to deliver your dress rehearsals with the technology and setup you will be using on speech day whether your presentation is in person, online, or hybrid.*

Do not forget to bring your stopwatch and remain aware of timing. It can take longer to deliver a speech with a microphone, particularly in a location with an echo. Also note that it generally takes longer to deliver a presentation before a live audience because you pause while listeners react and engage. Plan to have a time cushion; 10 percent of the total allotted time for the speech is usually sufficient.

On a final note, you cannot cram rehearsals for a presentation. It almost never worked for exams in school, and cramming all six rehearsals into the day (or night) before a presentation will not work either. One or two rehearsals a day during the week leading up to your presentation is a good goal and will help establish long-term memories that you can recall even when nervous. For longer, high-profile, and high stakes presentation, start even earlier and do more rehearsals.

Following a rehearsal schedule of at least six rehearsals may sound excessive, but it will mean the difference between feeling unsure and delivering a lackluster presentation or feeling confident and speaking dynamically during your next speaking role.

APPLICATION

Rehearse a presentation six times and conduct one technical dress rehearsal in the seven days leading up to a presentation. Write down a short reflection describing how you felt after each rehearsal. Compare how you felt after your first rehearsal and your last. How did your preparation impact your level of confidence and your performance in your actual presentation?

CHECKLIST FOR PRESENTATION DAY

You have done the hard work of crafting and rehearsing a great speech. Don't leave anything to chance on the day of your presentation. Here is a checklist to ensure you have everything you need to deliver a personal-best presentation whether the speaking situation is in person, online, or hybrid:

ALL PRESENTATIONS:

- ☐ List of stretches and vocal warm ups (see chapter 2 for details)
- ☐ Water bottle with room temperature water
- ☐ Light snack (such as fruit, an energy bar, or a bagel)
- ☐ Mints (and not gum)
- ☐ Medicine you may need (for headaches, upset stomach, etc.)
- ☐ Grooming supplies (comb, mirror, lip balm, makeup, stain remover, static sheet, etc.)

IN-PERSON PRESENTATIONS:

- ☐ Notes and props you will use at the lectern
- ☐ A professional-looking folder to hold your Sandwich Structure, notes, etc.
- ☐ Your slides or other supporting material in an electronic format (remember to send a copy to your easily accessible e-mail account as a backup)
- ☐ Handouts, brochures, and other materials you plan to make available to your audience
- ☐ Evaluation sheet (if you plan to get written feedback from your audience)
- ☐ Video camera and related equipment (if you plan to record your speech and / or get audience responses to your speech on video)
- ☐ Business cards
- ☐ Pen (but don't take it with you to the lectern)
- ☐ A belt or clothing with a waistband to affix a lavalier microphone

ONLINE PRESENTATIONS:

- ☐ Outline or notes you will use during your presentation
- ☐ Tape to affix outline or notes to a wall or place that allows you to keep your chin high
- ☐ Files, links, or QR codes for your slides, handouts, or evaluation form (and share with a producer or co-facilitator ahead of time)
- ☐ Headset, external microphone, webcam, laptop, power cord, Ethernet cable for Internet, green screen if using a virtual background, firm chair without wheels or a high back, computer stand or thick books to set your laptop on, and artificial lighting
- ☐ Phone with tripod or tablet with stand that is cellular enabled as a backup if Internet fails
- ☐ Phone numbers of the event organizer, producer, and/or co-facilitator in case of technical difficulties
- ☐ Draft email for participants with instructions for a backup videoconference or rescheduled session in the event of technical issues
- ☐ Stress relief or fidget toy that is silent and can be used outside camera range

HYBRID PRESENTATIONS:

- ☐ Painters tape to mark the speaking area that enables online participants to see the presenter
- ☐ See all lists above

Chapter 18

PARTICIPATING: MEETINGS, SMALL TALK, AND IMPROMPTU SPEAKING

The most overlooked element of presenting is the speaking we do as participants of routine meetings and conversations. In fact, many professionals claim that they "never present," despite often making contributions in meetings, engaging in workplace conversations, and responding off-the-cuff to questions from clients who call on the phone or colleagues who drop by their office.

If we are not running the meeting or listed on the agenda, it is quite easy to avoid the time, energy, and potential stress of preparing to participate. Precisely because of this, we under-prepare. The result can be feelings of frustration that we did not speak up at all or that our contributions were not clearer and more meaningful. A small amount of preparation can go a long way toward making your participation in meetings, conversations, and seemingly inconsequential speaking roles powerful sites for sharing your perspectives, bolstering your personal brand, improving communication outcomes, and advancing your career.

This chapter is devoted to sharing tips for preparing to participate and for speaking confidently in the moment.

Participating Is Presenting

Before entering a meeting of any format, remind yourself that participating is presenting. If you are virtual, write a note to yourself and stick it on the side of your computer monitor. Maybe you write "Smile" or "Energy" or "Be Clear" or "Be Concise." These might be the same notes you write to yourself if you were delivering prepared remarks. That's good!

If you are in person, a deep breath in your office before walking down the hall might help to put you in the right mindset. For any format, take a few minutes to review the agenda and materials for the meeting even though you are not responsible for presenting them. The key is to make yourself aware that this communication environment might require you to speak. This alone will move you toward more meaningful participation.

These may seem like small actions, but they might save you from embarrassment. A client of ours who works in sales shared a story about interviewing for a new position within the company. The hiring group had previously used panel interviews, with five panelists asking questions to one applicant. Recently, they shifted to one-on-one interviews. Those five people could no longer rely on each other to generate questions or piggie back on what others asked an applicant. When the panelist joined the meeting, they were shocked to see they were in a videoconference call alone with only the applicant—no panel. They forgot the new format. The panelist said, "I'm sorry but I've got nothing prepared. I thought we still did panels."

Getting into the habit of mentally preparing to participate would have provided the panelist with something to say. Instead, they approached the meeting passively. To actively contribute, you start with a mindset to actively participate.

You might also challenge yourself to speak up in the first ten minutes of a meeting. The number ten is arbitrary and can be longer or shorter depending on the speaker, audience, and occasion. Whatever that number of minutes is for you, contributing early on will help alleviate the stress of presenting and will also improve the likelihood that you will participate more than once in the meeting. If you tend to speak too much or interrupt others, identify an arbitrary number of speakers that must contribute after you before you jump in again.

Prepare Contributions

Do not wait for a meeting facilitator to assign you a speaking role. Ask in advance for time on the agenda to provide an update or share a perspective. Selecting and framing your topic proactively is always easier than adapting reactively. If the facilitator has no role or time on the agenda for you, still consider key issues you would like to raise, valuable insights you can share, and questions you need answered so you have contributions at the ready.

> *Do not wait for a meeting facilitator to assign you a speaking role.*

Also consider questions that could come your way. Brainstorm the three most likely questions and the three worst-case-scenario questions you could be asked during the meeting. Crafting a simple Sandwich Structure Outline (see chapter 5) and rehearsing your contribution aloud several times will increase confidence and reduce wordiness and tangents (see chapter 17). You can take this same proactive approach of preparing and practicing mini-outlines, so you don't feel unprepared during a Q&A session after a presentation, a panel presentation, and even conversations at the office water cooler.

Now that you are in a participatory mindset and have contributions ready to share, here is a method for responding to questions in the moment that will allow you to present concisely and confidently—even when responding to topics you did not anticipate.

Pause

When it is your turn to speak or a question is directed at you, give yourself a moment to process and breathe before speaking. Many professionals rush to answer without taking a moment to think it through. A three-second pause is perfectly acceptable, makes you appear confident, and will help prevent a rambling response. In virtual contexts, the time it takes you to unmute yourself is a helpful reminder to pause. Communication is irreversible. It is far better to have a noticeable pause and a strong response than an immediate answer that you regret.

Polite

Remember to show gratitude to the person asking you a question. This might be nonverbal—a slight crinkle at the eyes and upturn at the corners of the lips.

If you need more time to formulate your response, verbally thank the questioner. There is no one right way to do this. It might be, "Thank-you for asking about . . ." or "I'm so glad you brought up the issue of . . ." You need not say thank-you for each and every question in a long meeting or Q&A session, but you can use this strategy for questions you did not anticipate ahead of time.

You can also use gratitude to diffuse hostility by highlighting points where you agree. For example, "Thank-you for your question. I too am disappointed with the timeline for this project." Do not repeat the negative charge or accusation. Instead, pick out the issue being addressed. For example, "Thank-you for bringing up the issue of cost because I know it's a real concern in this economy." Another subtle way to show gratitude and respect is to respond to the questioner by name during your answer.

Paraphrase

Speakers should repeat or paraphrase questions to show they understand. If you are unclear about what was asked, don't hesitate to request clarification from the questioner. Repetition of questions during in-person events allows the speaker to share on microphone so everyone in the audience knows what was asked. In an online situation where listeners may be distracted, repeating questions allows everyone to focus on what was asked. Restating the question can also be helpful because you can reframe it when necessary—to diffuse a hostile question or to bridge the question to a related subject you want to discuss. Be careful when linking a question to another topic—it has to be in the ballpark or listeners will feel insulted.

Finally, honesty is the best policy; if you don't know, don't try to fake it. When appropriate, crowdsource a response by asking others in the meeting if they can answer. If there are no other subject-matter experts to rely on, you might give a provisional response such as, "Based on the information I have, this is what I think."

If you truly need more time, offer to follow up with the questioner with specific information that you don't know off the top of your head or that falls outside your area of expertise. Here are several ways to punt on a question, note they identify a timeline by which and format in which a response will be delivered:

- "I want to be sure to give you correct information. Let me call you back with the details this afternoon."

- "That's a good question. I'll see what I can find out for you by the close of business today."

- "I've been wondering that, too. Let me research today and report back by 10 a.m. tomorrow morning. Would you prefer to hear back by phone or email?"

Point

Just like a speech should have a thesis, a response to a question should have a clear point. Because many professionals do not prepare for meetings or prepare for time to formulate a response by pausing, being polite, and paraphrasing, their answers lack a point, or it comes at the very end of the answer. Especially when communicating with busy clients and colleagues, you want to share your point early on. In military briefing communications, this is known as the BLUF (bottom line up front) and is meant to respect the valuable time of listeners by sharing the most essential information first.

Structure

Whether you are providing a status update, making a recommendation, or responding to a question, structure your meeting contributions. This is a best practice of longer presentations and should be applied in less formal speaking situations as well.

Support your position with one anecdote, or two points, reasons, or examples (at the very most, three points, reasons, or examples). You can rely on familiar patterns of arrangement, such as problem-solution; past, present, future; why, how, what; and Three Story Structure (learn more about these patterns in chapter 6). A structured meeting contribution might sound something like:

- "Let me share one story to illustrate why this is the best option for our organization."

- "There are two reasons why our investment in the program is higher than expected. The first is . . ."

- "To understand this project, let me give you a brief summary of what we did last year, what we are doing now, and where we are headed next year."

Structure will enhance clarity—it will make your presentation easier to follow. Listeners will know what to expect and can more readily digest and retain what they hear. Structure will promote succinctness—by previewing what you will talk about, there is less chance you will go on tangents or lose your train of thought. Structure will elevate polish—meeting participants who are able to overview and then discuss one thoughtful story or a few key points when put on the spot come across as organized, prepared, and confident.

Short

Don't filibuster during meetings, especially online meetings with truncated agendas. Most updates and responses to questions should be short—about one to three minutes long. The length of your answer should depend first and foremost on how long it takes to fully answer the question. No need to stretch it past a sentence if that is all that is needed.

Summary

Just like a speech has a conclusion, a response to a question or a contribution in a conversation should have a summary that indicates to fellow meeting participants or conversational partners that you have finished your turn as a speaker. This is as simple as thanking the questioner and restating the question and thesis. In a conversational setting, it might include asking a question to keep the dialogue going.

Do not underestimate the importance of being a participant of meetings, conversations, and other informal speaking roles. Your contributions in these settings are presentations, and like formal public speeches, require planning, practice, and confidence for you to be the most effective speaker possible.

THREE P'S OF AVOIDING INTERRUPTIONS: PREVIEW, PITHY, AND PROJECT

Jean Miller, our colleague at Spoken with Authority, developed a three-part strategy to reduce the likelihood that you will be interrupted when speaking in a meeting or conversation. Here are her 3 P's of avoiding interruptions: Preview, Pithy, and Project.

- First, if you preview that you have two or three points or examples, people will be much less likely to dive in after the first one.

- Second, being pithy, or clear and concise, will give others less opportunity and less motivation to interrupt you. Keep your contributions short and to the point.

- Finally, project your voice to make it harder for others to speak over you. It is much easier to interrupt someone who is speaking softly than someone who is projecting their voice and/or using a quality microphone to amplify their voice.

Preview your points, keep it pithy, and project your voice to avoid having others interrupt you. And remember, the act of interrupting can be perceived differently depending on the context, the cultural backgrounds of the individuals who are interacting, and even based on conversational norms that vary by geographic region. Sometimes people interrupt to dominate a conversation, and that might rightly be perceived as rude behavior. Other times, people might excitedly jump in to support or add to the speaker's ideas. Deborah Tannen talks about "cooperative overlapping" which is a form of interruption that shows enthusiasm and builds on what the other person is saying.[1] When you think of interruptions in this way, you realize that you don't have to take being interrupted personally. Still, some people tend to get interrupted more than others, and learning how to maintain your speaking turn to complete your message can elevate your confidence and your professional demeanor.

Notes:

1. Deborah Tannen, "Turn-Taking and Intercultural Discourse and Communication," in *The Handbook of Intercultural Discourse and Communication*, ed. Christina Bratt Paulston, Scott F. Kiesling, Elizabeth S. Rangel (West Sussex, UK: Blackwell, 2012), 135-157.

Chapter 19

FACILITATING: MEETINGS

In March 2022, Microsoft published its annual Work Trends Index based on a survey of over 30,000 professionals. Results showed that, "Since February 2020, the average [Microsoft] Teams user saw a 252% increase in their weekly meeting time and the number of weekly meetings has increased 153%."[1] With this astonishing increase in meetings, it is vital for facilitators to be more selective in scheduling meetings and more productive when they do make the calendar. This chapter will help facilitators achieve these goals by taking a public-speaking approach to the planning and execution of in-person, virtual, and hybrid meetings.

Make Sure It is Necessary

Savvy speakers know that not every invitation to speak is worth accepting. Similarly, determine whether you need to hold a meeting to reach your objective. Is the spoken word necessary to achieve your objective? Could it be a pre-recorded video? Would a memo or e-mail do the trick?

> *Determine whether you need to hold a meeting to reach your objective.*

If you want to brainstorm ideas, get real-time feedback, or collaborate on a solution to a complex problem, assembling a group of people online or in person and using tools like a whiteboard makes sense. If you are engaging in one-way communication to make an announcement or inform stakeholders about a new procedure or process, consider sending a memorandum or pre-recorded tutorial instead. Hint: if there is only one speaker on the meeting agenda, it likely is one-way communication and not worthy of convening a meeting.

Analyze Your Audience

Just as you should research your audience before crafting a presentation, research the people who will be participating in your meeting—and only include people who really need to be there. If you do not already know expected participants, find out about their background and issues of interest from their company biography, online profiles, media reports, and even information you can glean from trusted friends and colleagues. When you do know expected participants, take time to find out what they want to discuss, what their perspective is on issues being discussed, what they would like to get from or contribute to the meeting, and what accommodations they require to participate fully. Incorporate participants into the meeting agenda ahead of time to highlight diverse perspectives and provide preparation time for individuals who are less comfortable speaking off-the-cuff.

When possible or appropriate, find out about dissent or problems before the meeting so you can take action or, at the very least, be prepared to address such issues during the meeting. As a presenter and meeting facilitator, you never want to be caught unprepared. The fewer surprises, the smoother your meeting will run. Be proactive by giving agenda time to dissenters to express their views. This can help bring to light overlapping perspectives and goals, providing a basis for constructive discussion.

Adapt to Your Audience

Effective speakers adapt their presentation based on an analysis of their listeners. It is not about pandering, but about being aware of and respecting audience member needs. When planning meetings, this means considering the best way for participants to get together. For online meetings, understand videoconference platform preferences for people you are inviting. Take time to understand if security protocols limit the ability of meeting participants to use certain platforms and videoconference features.

Avoid hybrid meetings—those where some participants are in person and others are online. The online participants often become an afterthought to the people in the room. Remote attendees are often members of marginalized groups, such as people with caregiving responsibilities, disabilities, or mobility challenges, to name a few. Hold routine and last-minute meetings entirely online to improve inclusiveness.

> *Avoid hybrid meetings. Hold routine and last-minute meetings entirely online to improve inclusiveness.*

Schedule in-person gatherings purposefully and far in advance. Take care to optimize the agenda and attendee experience to seize the opportunity for rapport building and social connection. When a hybrid meeting cannot be avoided, have co-equal facilitators—one online and one in person—so that all attendees receive attention and have opportunities to engage. Carefully test AV and IT capabilities so that in-person attendees can clearly see and hear online attendees and vice versa.

Try to accommodate attendee schedules. Remember that nobody wants to be invited to a meeting at 5:00 p.m. on a Friday afternoon, at 2 a.m. in their local time zone, or on the day of a religious observance. Take care to make scheduling inclusive of all meeting attendees. If time zone differences require inconvenient meeting times, the inconvenience should be shared and should not fall on the same person or group every single time.

After meeting details are set, send a meeting invite with the subject, time, location, agenda, attendees, etc. Also, a reminder e-mail is in order if you schedule your meeting more than a few days in advance.

Have a Thesis

Similar to a speech, a meeting requires a general purpose and thesis. Do you want to brainstorm? Make a decision? Get a status update? Is the purpose informative in nature or is it meant to persuade stakeholders to take a specific action? What information needs to be shared or what decision needs to be made for the meeting to be successful? Make sure the purpose is clear and your goal is limited in scope.

Make It Short

TED curator Chris Anderson famously said that TED Talks are limited to 18 minutes because it is "short enough to hold people's attention, including on the Internet, and precise enough to be taken seriously. But it's also long enough to say something that matters."[2] Applied to meetings, it doesn't mean that every meeting must be 18 minutes or less. But it is a reminder that humans have limited attention spans—and perhaps even shorter in computer-mediated contexts.

> *Humans have limited attention spans—and perhaps even shorter in computer-mediated contexts.*

Some organizations are now limiting all meetings to 30 minutes. Others are reducing 30-minute meetings to 25 minutes and 60-minute meetings to 45 minutes. No matter your approach to reducing meeting fatigue, set standards for meeting length and be ruthless about limiting meeting goals and number of attendees to respect time constraints. Remember that online meetings should always be shorter than the same one planned for an in-person format.

Have an Agenda

Presentations usually have two or three main points that support the thesis. So too should a meeting. Prepare an outline (see chapter 5 on the Sandwich Structure Outline) to identify the key issues you will discuss and decide how much time you will devote to each issue. This is your meeting agenda.

To lengthen the time listeners stay engaged, delegate speaking roles. Each time a new presenter speaks up or appears on the computer screen, audience members tend to refocus. Let speakers know their role in advance, including how long they will have for their contribution, so they can prepare. Share your agenda with all meeting participants ahead of time in the calendar invite or via e-mail. You might even use screen share to display it during online meetings. Include how much time you will spend on each agenda item to avoid a meeting that runs late.

Practice

Most presenters acknowledge they should rehearse before delivering a speech, though few do enough (see chapter 17 for more on how to rehearse effectively). But it never occurs to most facilitators to practice their contributions to a meeting.

If you want to come across as confident, polished, and professional in a speech or a meeting, you should rehearse. Just because you are sitting down at a conference table at your office or in your home and speaking to a small group online does not mean you can or should wing it. After all, the stakes can be particularly high at intimate meetings such as job interviews, performance evaluations, and client pitches.

> *If you want to come across as confident, polished, and professional in a speech or a meeting, you should rehearse.*

Aim to practice six times for success; this is the point when the material will stick and you won't struggle to recall what you want to say next or stumble over the wording of what you say. This is when you will be polished and professional. Do a technical rehearsal with the technology you will use during the actual meeting.

Command the Room

Just as there are many parallels between planning a meeting and crafting a presentation, speakers are well served to apply principles of effective presentation delivery when leading meetings. (See chapter 10 for tips on elevating your executive presence.) The following suggestions are specific to delivering the content of your meeting effectively:

When approaching the lectern, a confident speaker has great posture; moves slowly and purposefully; smiles; makes eye contact with members of the audience; starts with a loud, clear voice; and opens with a carefully crafted introduction rather than junk words like "um" or "so." Facilitators may not take their place on a stage or at a lectern, but they still need to command the room when they start a meeting. For online meetings, turn on your camera and upgrade from your computer's built-in microphone to a wired external microphone.

> *For online meetings, turn on your camera and upgrade from your computer's built-in microphone to a wired external microphone.*

Your command of the room—either online or in person —must continue throughout the meeting. If a participant is straying from the topic at hand, speaking too long or dominating the conversation, it is your responsibility to interrupt politely but firmly to get the meeting back on track or to include other attendees.

Start Strong and on Time

Memorable public speakers hook audience members with a catchy opening line. When leading a meeting, make sure to start purposefully too. Different leaders will open in different ways depending on their personality, leadership style, and type of meeting they are running. Some ideas for openings are giving out an award, recognizing a professional or personal achievement of a participant, sharing a topical and inspirational quotation, telling a humorous and relevant story, doing a round of introductions (including pronouns each participant uses to be inclusive), or engaging attendees with an icebreaker question or exercise. While meetings should be efficient, they should not be impersonal. Make an effort to establish rapport or build a team.

Whatever you do to open a meeting, do it on time. Starting late suggests that the meeting is disorganized or that the agenda will not be followed closely. Even if key players are not present, start. If you don't, they will continue to come late and waste the time of everyone else involved. If you do start on time, latecomers will get the message.

> *Starting late suggests that the meeting is disorganized or that the agenda will not be followed closely.*

For face-to-face meetings, arrive early to get set up and engage in friendly banter as attendees arrive. For online meetings, set up a virtual waiting room so you can admit participants and greet them a few minutes before the appointed start time.

Signpost

Great speeches have some set-up material after the catchy opening sentence, and so too should a meeting. After you open, make sure to state the purpose of the meeting so everyone is on the same page, even if participants didn't review the agenda in advance.

Give participants signposts, or a roadmap of what the meeting is about and how it will unfold. It is especially important to set out clear expectations as to the order of speakers, how participants will be recognized, how long they can speak, and how they will be interrupted if they go over or stray from the subject at hand. You might set "ground rules," such as limiting distractions and turning on cameras for online meetings. Communicating expectations can prevent meetings that run over time or fail to meet objectives as well as regulating overactive or underactive participants.

Have a clear transition from one issue to the next. If a participant is talking too long or getting off topic, follow through with your promise to interrupt and get the meeting back on track. It isn't rude when you've laid out expectations and hold all participants to the same standards. On the contrary, failing to interrupt would be rude to other participants who were promised a meeting on certain issues in a certain timeframe.

To interrupt, wait until the speaker is finishing a sentence or taking a breath (believe it or not, every speaker will breathe at some point), then pleasantly say, "Thank-you for bringing up that important issue. It's not on our agenda today, so after the meeting, I'll be in touch with you to set a time for the two of us to discuss it further. Right now, it's time to move on to the second item on today's agenda" or "Let's table this topic until our next meeting so we can make a decision on how to move forward this week."

As you would review main points before the conclusion of a speech, the end of the meeting should include a recap for each agenda item, the steps participants decided to take, noting who will take the lead, as well as how and when they will report back. Consider using a whiteboard or an online document that participants can edit and access simultaneously to save time and make sure everyone is on the same page.

End on Time

You gain goodwill by ending a presentation a few minutes early. Similarly, try to end your meeting a little early and never late. Meeting participants respect facilitators who respect their time. Remember to thank participants. If another meeting is scheduled or needs to be scheduled, confirm a date, time, and, location.

By applying best practices of crafting and delivering effective presentations to meetings, you can ensure your meetings will be well organized and productive, as well as reducing the ballooning number of meetings and hours spent in them.

MEETING OBSERVATION, CONSTRUCTION, AND REFLECTION

Observation:
When attending an upcoming meeting, ask yourself the following questions about the delivery style of the leader and other speakers: What communicative behaviors help the meeting run smoothly? Which ones hinder the flow of the meeting? Which ones establish authority of the speaker? Which undermine it? How did the facilitator manage difficult moments or personalities in the meeting?

Construction:
When preparing to facilitate an important upcoming meeting, use a Sandwich Structure Outline a week in advance to develop your agenda and practice your speaking roles six times in the days leading up to the meeting.

Reflection:
After facilitating, reflect on how the meeting went. What was accomplished? How effectively did you make use of the opportunity for two-way communication and for building community? How did you feel when facilitating?

Notes:
1. "Great Expectations: Making Hybrid Work *Work*," *Microsoft Work Trend Index 2022*, March 16, 2022, https://bit.ly/3AwjxAx

2. Carmine Gallo, "Neuroscience Proves You Should Follow TED's 18-Minute Rule to Win Your Pitch," *Inc.*, accessed May 11, 2022, https://bit.ly/3CcpBzp

Chapter 20

INFORMING: BRIEFINGS AND REPORTS

I nformative speaking needs a better publicist. For too long, briefings and reports have been wrongfully equated with being boring, bland, plain, and uninteresting.

But informing is fundamental to all speaking. If you are persuading, you are also informing an audience about a problem in order to move them in support of the solution you are suggesting. If you are entertaining, the examples and stories that you share are the information that makes the speech funny, memorable, and poignant. If you are interviewing for a job, the information that you provide about you and your experiences is what will make you seem like a good fit for the position.

> *Informing is fundamental to all speaking.*

The following strategies are not format specific; they apply to in-person, virtual, and hybrid situations. One could argue that compelling information is even more important for virtual and hybrid presentations, wherein it is easier for audience members to become distracted due to lack of in-person accountability. If we are being honest, we should assume that we need to make compelling informative presentations regardless of format.

Employ the following strategies to make your material memorable and useful the next time you explain a new process or pressing issue, provide an update on a project, or report research findings.

Give Your Audience a Reason to Care

Consider why your message is important to your audience. Ask the all-important WIIFM question: "What's in it for me?" The "me" in this question is the listener, not the presenter! Humans are selfish; we want to know how we will benefit personally from listening to a presentation. The central idea should be crafted to be directly relevant to audience members.

An informative presentation is not about what you want to discuss—it is about what listeners need to know. To identify what your audience needs to know, spend time analyzing your audience, their interests, and needs. (See chapter 3 for more about analyzing the audience and occasion.)

One way to approach informative speaking is to explain to your audience these four N's about your subject:

- What is **new** to the audience (even if it's not new to you)

- What is **now** or current about it

- Something they **need** to know

- Something that is **neat** to know

See the sidebar in chapter 6 for patterns of arrangement well suited to informative presentations.

Stay Focused on the Listener and out of the Weeds

When conducting briefings, fight the impulse to include everything. Instead, focus on one thing—the one thing that is most crucial for listeners to know when you stop speaking. It may be tempting, but refrain from trying to teach listeners everything you know on a topic. You want to give them the highlights that are most applicable to them. For example, listeners don't need to know how a new computer system works, they just need to know how to use the elements of it relevant to their position. Remember, a presentation should be about providing value to listeners, not demonstrating how much you know. People who want more detail can always ask during Q&A or talk with you one-on-one at a later time.

When determining what to include and exclude, remember that online briefings and reports, and any virtual presentation for that matter, should include half the material and take half the time you would spend on that presentation at an in-person conference or meeting.

Incorporate a Theme

Particularly for dry or abstract topics, introduce a theme that you can weave throughout your informative speech. This introduces a humanistic element that will be memorable and serve as the foundation for interesting visual aids. A theme will also help avoid the "info dump," whereby a speaker unloads a vast quantity of information on their audience all in the name of being informative. If your audience cannot track your presentation or tunes out, is it worth "covering" certain material?

For example, an HR professional prepared a speech for colleagues on an important reporting process that they only had to complete a few times a year. An avid pianist, she linked each part of the process she was describing to one of her favorite piano pieces. Her listeners will never forget to submit their completed information with the online form . . .and hear Scott Joplin's "The Entertainer" in their heads while they do it. A good theme does not have to be overtly related to the content of the speech. The metaphor or analogy you use should, however, be creatively linked to the material, carried throughout the presentation, and true to your personality.

WHEN AND HOW TO USE HANDOUTS

Handouts can be a useful supplement to an informative speech. However, it is best practice to think long and hard about the necessity of using a handout. Forgo handouts for a short or straightforward informative speech and send an electronic follow-up after the session. Announce your intention to do so at the start of your briefing or report so audience members can focus on listening rather than writing.

If you decide that a handout is important to supplement a longer or more complicated briefing with slides, think carefully about what to include and how to format it. When remote participants are using their own paper and toner to print materials, you want to avoid large colored images, dark backgrounds, and lengthy documents. Limit pages and share in a PDF file to preserve your formatting across computers and to protect your intellectual property. Distribute your handout electronically well in advance so it can be interpreted, translated, and/or printed by remote participants. For handouts you print and bring to in-person events, it is still a good idea to limit pages and print double-sided to save paper. Distribute materials before you speak to avoid needless distractions.

Include in your handout:

- Signposts, but not a script. Provide enough material for the audience to follow your presentation and take useful notes, but not so much that they could read it and replace listening to you. Handouts should supplement, not replace, the speaker. You can always provide a full written report on your topic, but this should not be confused with the presentation's visuals aids and supporting handout.

- Room for notes. People will remember more if they can jot down ideas and put concepts in their own words,

- Reproductions of visuals. If you have a complicated graph or other visual, include it in your handout so audience members can study it up close while you are explaining it.

- Additional resources. Because you cannot and should not cover everything in an informative presentation, a handout is an ideal way to tell attendees how to reach you for more information. Consider including a phone number, e-mail address, and social media channels you use professionally. A handout is an excellent resource to share places to learn more on the topic, such as websites, books, articles, films, videos, etc. You can also include a full report or appendices that have more detail than you give justice to during your presentation. Your handout does not have to be an exact replica of your slides (and in most cases should not be the same).

Have Vivid Supporting Material

Briefings often get bogged down with statistics and facts. To help your audience make sense of the information and retain it, incorporate humanistic supporting material. For example, balance a statistic with a compelling story about a person who exemplifies it. Following are techniques that bolster storytelling and human connection:

- Analogies: Can you explain something from the present in terms of a previous, similar situation?

- Metaphors: Can you explain a complex or unknown idea in terms of something familiar?

- Hypotheticals: Can you create a composite figure to humanize what aggregate data explains?

- Processes: Can you explain how something works or the impact of a decision, step-by-step to make it real to listeners?

- Localization: Can you take a national or state-wide trend and illustrate its impact on a city, town, organization, neighborhood, school, or other group the audience would understand?

Use pictures, images, props, video clips, and other audio-visual aids to make your supporting material even more concrete. Watch Joe Smith's TED Talk entitled, "How to Use a Paper Towel" to see how props and demonstration can make an informative presentation more memorable. Remember, when listeners hear a narrative or see a new and interesting image on their computer screen, they refocus attention. (See chapter 9 for more on presentation aids.)

Do Not End with Q&A

Many informative presentations have a question-and-answer period at the end. While entertaining questions is particularly useful to help engage listeners, you never want to end a presentation on an audience question as it might be irrelevant or hostile. Take questions after you review your main points and before your conclusion. After Q&A ends, repeat your review and share concluding remarks, which should call back to the interesting concept you opened with. (See chapter 7 for more on introductions and conclusions.)

By keeping your next briefing or report short, audience-centric, and concrete, your next informative presentation will be more likely to hold the attention of listeners, meet its objectives, and might just improve the reputation of informational presentations.

Chapter 21

TEACHING: WEBINARS AND WORKSHOPS

Many professionals do not consider themselves teachers by trade, but as their areas of expertise develop, they will surely be called upon to educate others. Such opportunities may come by way of training programs for colleagues or clients, members of a professional association, or participants at an industry conference. They may even present as opportunities to teach learners at a community center or instruct students at a local school, college, or university. With the rise of online education, opportunities to teach and the reach of training programs are increasing.

This chapter is dedicated to improving learning sessions. It will start with suggestions for planning an effective live webinar or on-site training program and include tips for an engaging delivery.

Use One Mode of Delivery

As recommended with meetings in chapter 19, avoid training programs where some participants are in person and others are online. Online participants are often an afterthought in this setup, and remote event attendees are often members of marginalized groups to begin with. Plan learning opportunities that are all online or all in person to help promote equity. If you must use a hybrid format, have co-equal trainers—one online and one in person to ensure all participants receive robust attention and have ample opportunities to engage.

Limit Time and Learning Outcomes

Learning outcomes tell participants what whey will be able to do after your session. Be careful not to fall into the trap of "covering all the material." It is far better to achieve depth of understanding and proficiency in a few topics rather than a superficial knowledge on many subjects. When presenting online, reduce the number of goals and length of the program because learners are more prone to distractions and likely to experience videoconference fatigue.

> *It is far better to achieve depth of understanding and proficiency in a few topics rather than a superficial knowledge on many subjects.*

For webinars where you have over 20 participants and cannot interact personally during the session, limit time to 60 minutes. For virtual workshops where you have 20 or fewer participants who you can personally interact with, you can present for 90 minutes up to two hours. The more exercises and active-learning techniques you incorporate, the longer your in-person or virtual workshop can be. Make sure to incorporate bathroom and movement breaks about every hour.

Keeping training sessions short and objectives limited is not an endorsement of single-dose training sessions. One-and-done learning events are common in professional settings, but almost unheard of at high schools and institutions of higher learning where semester-long courses are the norm. Instead of hosting random acts of training in the workplace, consider ways to make learning opportunities multi-session and cumulative so participants have a greater likelihood of building new skills and generalizing them to new contexts.[1]

Shift the Focus to Doing

Pedagogical methods long have centered on lecturing students—telling them what the instructor knows. In the late 20th century, there was a shift to demonstration—showing students what the instructor is talking about. Seeing and hearing is more engaging and improves recall compared to listening alone, but it still is passive learning. Active learning is far more engaging and effective.

Think back to your favorite teacher. Chances are your teacher did more than just stand in front of the classroom and read their notes or slides. They likely managed to involve you in the learning experience. Research supports this experiential approach.[2] In other words, trainers should aim to have learners do something rather than just telling and/or showing them how to do it.

> *Trainers should aim to have learners do something rather than just telling and/or showing them how to do it.*

Encourage active learning in webinars and training programs by crafting outcomes that start with action words such as create, solve, plan, design, assess, justify, prove, and apply. You can include some verbs that reference lower order thinking skills, such as identify, classify, list, describe, compare, explore, and report, but they should not make up the bulk of learning objectives.

There are many ways to promote active learning on webinars and virtual workshops (see sidebar). Incorporate one activity every ten minutes in online formats and one every 20 minutes in face-to-face situations to help maintain attention of learners.

Now that we have explored ways to plan effective learning programs, here are some tips to effectively deliver a live webinar or virtual training program.

Set Up Early and Start on Time

Do a technical check prior to the date of your training program and make needed adjustments to your plans, materials, and technology. On the day of the presentation, arrive or log-in at least 30 minutes early so you have ample time to set up and troubleshoot any technological problems. As participants start arriving, display information confirming the course and instructor.

Make several announcements to welcome participants and let them know that the session will soon get underway. Particularly in online formats, you don't want listeners to wait too long without verbal acknowledgement, whether on a slide or in the chat box. Start the program promptly at the appointed time to respect the time of audience members. You might make your introduction a little long to account for latecomers. (See chapter 7 on attention getters and introductions.)

Welcome and Orient Participants

After the session starts, continue to welcome participants who arrive a few minutes late. Do not scold latecomers. Be sure to welcome them warmly and get them up to speed by saying something brief, such as, "We're now taking a short pre-test. Here's a copy so you can fill it out" or "If you are just joining us, thanks for participating in our webinar on XYZ topic. If you would like to ask a question, please type it into the chat box and then click the submit button or use the raise-hand feature on the videoconference platform."

As the last example showed, you should tell participants how to interact. Based on your webinar platform or audience engagement technologies, you may also have other interactive tools at your disposal. Briefly highlight and demonstrate features you will use to keep your program interactive.

ACTIVE LEARNING TECHNIQUES

Below are strategies to help keep learners actively engaged in a workshop or webinar:

Polls and quizzes

Include polls to learn more about audience members' experiences and attitudes, as well as quizzes to check for understanding. Consider administering a pre-test at the beginning and post-test at the end to assess learning.

Participant feedback

Most webinar platforms have participant feedback icons, such as yes/no and thumbs up/thumbs down. For on-camera webinar participants and in-person sessions, attendees can use their hand to show a thumbs up/thumbs down or "fist to five." Fist to five is when participants hold up their fist or fingers to their level of agreement or disagreement with a statement. They hold up a fist for strong disagreement and by adding one finger at a time up to all five fingers, they can incrementally show their level of agreement.

Chat box

Put a prompt in the videoconference chat box or share an open-ended question in an audience engagement platform like Mentimeter, such as "The most useful insight I learned in the section was . . ." or "Today, I am feeling . . ." Participants can fill in their response to a substantive or icebreaker question in the chat box. A variation on using the chat box is the "waterfall method." Ask webinar participants a question that requires a one-word or numeric response, such as "What city are you from?" or "Enter your solution to equation #3 on your handout." Have participants type their answer in the chat box and hit "enter" at the same time so all the responses cascade down the chat box at the same time.

You can use the chat box to take questions from participants at regular intervals, ideally every 10 to 20 minutes. Some platforms offer direct messages or anonymous questions that increase the likelihood that shy or reluctant attendees will participate.

Whiteboard

If your training room has a whiteboard or your videoconference platform has an electronic whiteboard, ask participants to write one thing the instructor could have explained more clearly. Other participants can vote on questions by adding a star or check mark near the items that resonate with them most.

Think, pair, share

Pose a question, case study, scenario, or prompt and ask learners to think about it for a few moments. Then, assign pairs in the physical space or in breakout rooms on your videoconference platform to discuss the topic. Time permitting, you can put pairs into groups of four to continue the discussion. Finally, ask pairs or quads to report their responses and start a discussion among all session participants. This is particularly effective when used with scenarios, case studies, role-playing, and other prompts that foster high-order thinking.

Debate

Assign learners to support or oppose an issue. Have each team craft several arguments for their position, support each argument with evidence, and prepare rebuttals to likely objections from the other team. Time the presenters for each argument, then allow questions from the opposing team. Allow students who did not formally present an argument to serve as debate judges.

Be Especially Clear and Concrete

It is always important to strive for clarity in the structure, descriptions, explanations, and directions you provide during live learning sessions, either online, in person, or hybrid. This need is magnified in the case of prerecorded training modules because listeners can't ask for immediate clarification if they don't understand.

To highlight the structure of any webinar or virtual training, provide overt objectives as well as signposting. (See chapter 8 for more on signposting.) For descriptions and explanations, consider using a mix of analogies, metaphors, anecdotes, visual aids, demonstrations, and quotations to make your point concrete. To clarify directions, consider supplementing verbal instructions with written bullet points on slides and handouts so participants can hear and see each step.

Get Support

Ask any teacher, and they will tell you that managing any learning environment is difficult. It is even more difficult online because you not only have to command your content and engage learners, but you also have to navigate the videoconference platform and monitor the chat box. Ask the event organizer, emcee, IT professional, or a colleague to serve as a producer or co-facilitator for online training programs. Give that collaborator co-host status on the virtual platform so they can manage the waiting room to let participants and latecomers in, the chat box for pressing questions from listeners on technology glitches or learning content, and the overall videoconference platform for technical issues or Zoombombers. Provide your collaborator a copy of your slides so they can display them on the videoconference platform if your Internet becomes unstable or your technology otherwise fails; you can call in by phone to narrate the audio.

You may not consider yourself a teacher, but you can effectively share your expertise with others by planning focused and interactive content, and by following best practices of delivering online and in-person instruction.

Notes:

1. Deanna P. Dannels, Amy L. Housley Gaffney, "Communication Across the Curriculum and in the Disciplines: A Call for Scholarly Cross-curricular Advocacy," *Communication Education* 58, no. 1 (2009): 124-153.
2. Elise J. Dallimore, Julie H. Hertenstein, and Marjorie B. Platt, "Using Discussion Pedagogy to Enhance Oral and Written Communication Skills," *College Teaching* 56, no. 3 (2008): 163-172.

Chapter 22

PERSUADING: PITCHES AND RECOMMENDATIONS

If you are not in the sales profession, you might bristle at the thought of your presentation being called a "sales pitch." However, when you think about it, we all are salespeople in the best sense of the concept: we are trying to use our expertise to guide people to ideas, policies, services, and outcomes that are mutually beneficial. Some people might have sales in their job description, but we all do some degree of selling or persuading in our professional lives.

Because persuasion is both a common and crucial workplace presentation skill, this chapter will explore three powerful theories of persuasion and will outline the operational process to apply them to the structure of your next pitch.

Aristotle

One of the most celebrated treatises on persuasion is Aristotle's time-tested *Rhetoric*, which dates to the 4th Century BCE. Aristotle defined rhetoric as "The faculty of observing, in any given case, the available means of persuasion."[1] He continued to classify those available means of persuasion, focusing mainly on the three types of appeals that a speaker can make: ethos, pathos, and logos.

Appeals to ethos are ones that draw upon the speaker's credibility—their goodwill, good sense, and good moral character. Pathos refers to appeals to emotion, when speakers invite audience members to feel and imagine what they have experienced. And logos has to do with reasoning, specifically the structure and content of an argument.

Takeaway

Present-day speakers are well served to use Aristotle's classical concepts of ethos, pathos, and logos to craft balanced appeals in their persuasive pitches. All too often, presenters rely on facts, figures, and data (heavy on logos). They regularly ignore ethos and pathos, easily remedied by telling stories. Storytelling in virtual contexts is especially important because rapport is more difficult to build, and emotion is more difficult to convey. (See the speech introduction checklist on page 84.)

Monroe

Fast forward from antiquity to the 1930's when Alan Monroe, a professor at Purdue University, coined a structure for persuasive speeches. Called Monroe's Motivated Sequence, the five steps are: attention, need, satisfaction, visualization, and action.[2]

Attention

Effectively persuading listeners requires speakers to garner the attention of audience members at the outset of the presentation. (See chapter 7 for more on attention getters.) You are convincing audience members to change their minds or their behavior. If they are not engaged in the presentation from the beginning, it is highly unlikely you will sway them.

Need

After you get the attention of the audience, the second element of persuasion is establishing a need. You, as a presenter, need to demonstrate that there is a problem, gap, injustice, or some other deficiency that exists in the world today that impacts your audience members. Without a clear and pressing need, it is not likely that listeners will accept or approve your proposed solution.

Satisfaction

Provide a robust plan to solve the problem. That may seem obvious, but you would be surprised how many speakers construct doomsday scenarios and then offer the most inconsequential plans to satisfy that need. Provide enough detail to make the audience feel

PERSUADING: PITCHES AND RECOMMENDATIONS

comfortable that you have thought through how the need can be satisfied. You might give examples of similar solutions that have worked elsewhere. Also, make a point of showing that your solution is feasible. That's not to say that you shouldn't propose revolutionary ideas or think outside the box.

Visualization

Visualization is the process of helping your audience imagine the benefits that will come after the need is satisfied. This involves painting a picture of what the world will look like with the solution enacted. Compelling solutions often have broader benefits than solving the stated problem. For example, curb cuts at intersections make streets accessible to people who use wheelchairs. They are also helpful for people who use canes, walkers, and other mobility devices, not to mention people with strollers or travelers with wheeled suitcases. Help your listeners see in their mind's eye all the benefits your solution can offer.

Action

The final step in Monroe's Motivated Sequence is telling audience members what specifically they can do to enact the solution. The action step should be tailored to the audience and should seem somewhat easy to accomplish. If you are strengthening or weakening the bond between listeners and a position, then the action step might be a statement of what they need to remember or take away from your presentation. If you are advocating a new program, the action step may be approving a budget, contacting one's representative in a legislative body, or casting a vote in an upcoming referendum.

Takeaway

Persuasive speakers can use the five steps of Monroe's Motivated Sequence to structure their thoughts in a range of speaking situations—from a formal presentation to a casual conversation. They should also remember the importance of thinking of a proposal's benefits in terms of the listener (not themselves). This step is easy to overlook in online persuasive speeches because the audience is not physically present, and depending on the videoconference platform, may not appear on the speaker's computer screen at all. Audience members you are hoping to persuade want to know, "What's in it for me?" An instinct for self-preservation lies deep within everyone; people care first and foremost about themselves. Accordingly, if you want to land a new job, don't focus on how much you will learn and grow professionally in the position. Instead, tell the interviewer how you will give them peace of mind, make their life easier, provide creative solutions to problems, or even make them look good to higher ups.

The Conversion Myth

The Conversion Myth refers to the common and mistaken belief that the sole purpose of persuasion is to convert a person from one belief to another. In fact, conversion is just one persuasive purpose—one that can be made more difficult in virtual and hybrid situations because attention spans are short and it is more difficult to build rapport. There are other persuasive purposes, and it is important to remember that a persuasive presentation can be successful even if it is not intended to change the attitudes or actions of listeners.

Other than conversion, a presenter may seek to **strengthen the bond** between the audience and an idea or behavior. Listeners who already share your views or already behave the way that you are asking them to behave can be persuaded to become more committed to that view or behavior.

Another persuasive purpose can be to **weaken the bond** between an audience and their ideas or behaviors. In general, humans are resistant to change. If you cannot change a listeners' attitudes or actions at that moment, you at least want to deliver a presentation that shows the benefits of your position. This might weaken the bond between the listener and their commitment to their original position. In weakening that bond, you've created a potential opening for the future.

Lastly, a presenter's purpose might be to **encourage a specific action**. Encouraging action may contain elements of conversion, strengthening a bond, or weakening a bond. What makes this persuasive purpose distinct is that you are asking the audience to do something, such as send an e-mail, cast a vote, approve an expenditure, or make a donation. In some ways, this can be the most difficult persuasive purpose because you are asking the audience to give up a scarce resource—time or money. Encouraging a specific action can be difficult, which is why understanding persuasive structure is important.

Hidden among these three strategic purposes is a relational dimension to persuasion. In nearly every situation, you want your audience to think highly of you even if the outcome is not what you were hoping for. If you are pitching for business or talking about policy with a legislator, you might not land a new client or win a sponsor for a bill, but the manner in which you conduct yourself keeps open the chance of future interactions.

Structuring Persuasive Messages

How do these persuasive theories apply to an occasion where you are making recommendations, pitching a product or service, or advocating?

Monroe's Motivated Sequence has the most direct link to your persuasive speech outline. (See chapter 5 for more on outlining presentations.) As described, the five elements of that persuasive process are, in order: attention, need, satisfaction, visualization, and action. In other words, the main points in the body of a speech where you are making recommendations could be:

1. Need

2. Solution

3. Benefits

This structure is particularly helpful when you have a strong sense of the listeners' needs, but that is not always the case. Even if everyone in the room is very clear on the problem, it may not merit that much real estate in the body of the presentation. Here are two alternatives that don't focus on the problem section in the body of the speech.

The Golden Circle

Articulated in his September 2009 TEDxPuget Sound speech and his 2011 book *Start with Why: How Great Leaders Inspire Everyone to Take Action*, Simon Sinek argues that great leaders and organizations inspire action by starting with why. In his schematic, "why" is at the core of the Golden Circle, the middle layer is the "how," and the outer ring is the "what." If you create a pitch outline based on his Golden Circle concept, the body of your speech would progress as follows:

1. Why

2. How

3. What

Sinek contends this is opposite of how several speakers and less successful businesses commonly organize their pitches, many of which (including boiler-plate pitch decks) are structured in the following way:

1. Who we are

2. What we do

3. What we can do for you

The problem is that, in most cases, the listener does not care who you are or what you do. They are only interested in what you can do for them—also known as the "why."

Three Story Structure

In chapter 8 on previews, reviews, and transitions, we mentioned Steve Job's famous June 2005 commencement address at Stanford University, where he opened with a self-deprecating joke and then previewed the body of his speech by saying, "Today I want to tell you three stories from my life. That's it. No big deal. Just three stories."

Although Jobs was not delivering a sales pitch or set of recommendations in a business meeting, it would be wise for persuasive speakers to emulate his structure that we have coined the "Three Story Structure." Instead of telling personal stories from their lives, however, persuasive speakers could share three success stories, case studies, client examples, testimonials, etc. These three narratives highlight the benefits experienced by three individuals or organizations that have collaborated with you and answers the all-important question: "What's in it for me?" (also known as "What we can do for you").

Under this organizational scheme, the body of a pitch would look like:

1. Success story 1

2. Success story 2

3. Success story 3

This pitch structure is the most "why" focused of the three alternatives suggested here and must be followed up in discussion, Q&A, and/or a formal proposal with more detail on how the work will get done, what will happen, who will do it, how much it will cost, etc. It is also the most narrative driven in keeping with Aristotle's advice to balance ethos and pathos with logos. Also, the main points are logically independent (as opposed to Monroe and Sinek whose structures are linked logically, so if one link in the chain fails to persuade, the entire presentation is not likely to be successful). In this scenario, if just one story resonates with listeners, they can be persuaded.

Process of Elimination

Some listeners prefer a clear and forceful recommendation. Others do not like to be told what to do. If you are speaking to listeners who fall in the latter category or who are reluctant or even hostile to your proposal, consider structuring your persuasive presentation using the process of elimination.

In this structure, the body of your speech would be:

1. Option 1

2. Option 2

3. Option 3

While presenting options, inform listeners about the pros and cons of each. Leave the most compelling option for last, allowing audience members to weigh the costs and benefits, hopefully coming to your conclusion on their own. You might even ask for feedback or take a vote after presenting options and before exploring next steps in your call to action. This approach can help build consensus and increase commitment to a decision because listeners decided on their own.

Ultimately, as a presenter, you need to do a thorough analysis of your audience and situation to determine an appropriate persuasive message and speech structure. Consider using Monroe's Motivated Sequence, The Golden Circle, Three Story Structure, or Process of Elimination to organize your next pitch speech and unequivocally answer for listeners: "What's in it for me?" No matter what you are trying to sell them or persuade them to do, do not start with the nuts and bolts (e.g., "who we are" or "what we'll do"). Be aware that in many instances, arguing for wholesale change may involve asking listeners to go further than they are ready or willing to go. And doing so could have the opposite impact, known as the Boomerang Effect, of making listeners more resistant to your proposal.[3]

All professionals engage in sales—whether they are pitching products and services, or persuading listeners to consider new ideas, adopt new approaches, approve a new budget request, kick off a new initiative, or strengthen or weaken bonds. Speakers are well-served when they are strategic and patient. The persuasive process is incremental and often lengthy. It is rarely accomplished in one presentation.

Notes:

1. Aristotle, *Rhetoric*, trans. W. Rhys. Roberts, ed. W.D. Ross (New York: Cosimo Press, 2010), 6.

2. Alan H. Monroe, *Principles and Types of Speech* (Glenview, IL: Scott Foresman, 1935). This is the first edition. The book has had many editions with various authors.

3. Carl Iver Hovland, Irving Lester Janis, and Harold H. Kelley, *Communication and Persuasion: Psychology Studies of Opinion Change* (New Haven, CT: Yale University Press, 1953).

Chapter 23

MODERATING: PANELS, GROUP PRESENTATIONS, AND INTRODUCING SPEAKERS

A common and costly mistake of panel moderators and leaders of group presentations is believing that less speaking time means less preparation time. On the contrary, moderating takes as much preparation time as giving the entire presentation yourself.

Jim Becker, an information technology director who spent years moderating panels as well as planning meetings and conferences, explains why this is the case. You are "like a great party host: making everyone feel welcome, knowing how to avoid or handle lulls, knowing how to get a conversation going between others, knowing how to rescue someone from an inappropriate or overly long conversation, and knowing how to wrap things up when it's time for the party to end—all done with alertness and diplomacy, and without expecting to be the center of attention."

Just like a great party requires careful preparation, so does a great panel or group presentation. Here is what a moderator/facilitator can do beforehand to ensure that guests—speakers and the audience—have a positive experience.

Analyze the Audience and Select Speakers

When preparing a panel or group presentation, the moderator and/or conference planner should identify the target audience. (See chapter 3 on analyzing the audience and occasion.) Aim to present a panel addressing a timely issue that falls at the intersection of what speakers know and what listeners care about. Along with the right topic, select the right panelists to ensure a successful event. Invite thought leaders and newsmakers who have credibility on the issue, as well as an important point of view. Aim to showcase a range of people and perspectives. Audience members, justifiably, are acutely aware when people from underrepresented groups are not included in panels and group presentations. Be proactive, intentional, and inclusive when you are inviting speakers.

Seek out panelists who are dynamic speakers; the best authorities on a topic do not always make the best panelists. Similarly, select speakers who are willing to present within the parameters (topic, time constraints, etc.) of the panel or group presentation.

It may be easier to go with the flow when it comes to audience analysis and speaker selection, but the mantra of The Mandalorian—"This is the way"—does not always apply. If something isn't working, it is okay to ask if there is another way. If, as an audience member, you have found yourself questioning why panel discussions are conducted in a certain way, then remember that sentiment when you are on the other side as a panelist and try to create the panel experience that you and your peers would like to see.

Share a Vision

Moderators are wise to connect with panelists well in advance to explain their vision for the panel or group presentation: what it is about, why speakers are included, what they should address to avoid repetition, how long they should speak, how the presentation or panel will unfold, how question and answer will proceed, what videoconference platform or AV setup you will use, and any other relevant details.

Listen to the suggestions of the speakers or panelists regarding your vision for the session. Be receptive to new ideas and flexible about making changes. Having an open dialogue about the panel or group presentation will help ensure an outline that is well-suited to participants, and who are comfortable with the focus of the session, as well as a successful final product.

Discuss the necessity of slides. If using visual aids, compile them in one file in advance to ensure compatibility and ease of transition. Provide clear guidance on speaking time, especially when you allow slides, so you don't run out of time for audience questions during your session. Make sure to exchange phone numbers so event planners and speakers can be reached last minute in case of travel delays or technological difficulties.

Craft an Agenda and Speaking Material

A panel or group presentation should have a detailed agenda, including the exact time that each element of the session will take place. Each speaker should receive a copy of the agenda ahead of time, so they know what to expect and how to prepare, such as opening remarks or responses to specific questions that the moderator plans to ask.

While an agenda is a good outline, the moderator of a panel or the facilitator of a group presentation must also prepare what he or she will say at certain points in the program. This speaking material does not need to be scripted; planned and rehearsed talking points often work well. Nevertheless, it remains vitally important to prepare and rehearse the following:

An Opening

Get the attention of audience members with a catchy fact, statistic, quotation, anecdote, or other compelling and relevant material. (See chapter 7 for more on attention-getting devices.) Then welcome the audience members (taking care to recognize online participants of hybrid events), thank panelists and speakers, link the opening line to the purpose of the session, and preview how the presentation will unfold (be explicit about when and how audience members can ask questions). Remember, for situations where some audience members are in person and others are joining remotely that both audiences need to have a method to ask questions that is closely monitored by a moderator or facilitator.

Introductions

Moderators and facilitators can craft the agenda so there is time to introduce all speakers during the beginning of the session or introduce each right before they present. Ask speakers to provide an introduction ahead of time. Most will send a page-long biography that must be shortened and made relevant to the panel discussion or group presentation. A good introduction is 30 to 60 seconds long, highlights the most interesting and important aspects of a speaker's credentials, and provides a teaser of his or her remarks. An introduction must also include the speaker's preferred title as well as the correct pronouns and pronunciation of each speaker and their affiliation(s). Practice out loud—it doesn't count to say it in your head!

Q&A and Conclusion

Plan in advance how and when you will solicit questions. Write down several questions ahead of time to ask as you wait for listeners to ask questions aloud or type questions in the chat box on the videoconference or audience engagement platform. You can also use your questions to keep the discussion going during a lull in audience questions. Consider asking a person or two in the audience you know and trust to raise a hand as soon as Q&A begins. This can encourage others to ask a question and keeps the tone of the event fast-paced and positive. It is not ideal to have a long, awkward silence when the floor is opened to audience questions.

Ten minutes before the end of the session, give notice that the panel is ending by calling for one more question from an audience member. After it is answered, pose a broad last question that allows each panelist to speak. Avoid asking a question that will rehash what has already been discussed. Instead, ask a final question about future trends or forward-looking advice. Then, thank the speakers, audience members, event organizers, panelists, and/or sponsors for providing a forum and engaging in a discussion on such an important issue. Share additional resources available to attendees and announce future events that may be of interest.

Link the conclusion to the catchy fact, statistic, quotation, or anecdote you led with in the opening. If you have an online evaluation form for the session, provide a paper copy, QR code, or link in the chat box (depending on the audience) and ask listeners to fill it out.

These are not show-up and wing-it speaking roles. Similar to the best hosts, these roles take a thoughtful approach to planning a party, or in this case, the panel presentation. For best results, approach moderating a panel or facilitating a group presentation as if you were delivering the entire presentation on your own—your careful preparation and confident delivery will set the stage for a successful ensemble.

PREPARE TO FACILITATE A DISCUSSION

Though effective moderators do much of their facilitating on the spot, they can practice relevant skills ahead of time, including:

Listening

Moderators need to listen carefully to interject follow-up questions, ask related questions of speakers who have not been as involved in the conversation, and smoothly transition from speaker to speaker and topic to topic.

Repeating and Reframing

Moderators must read questions from the chat box or restate questions asked by in-person attendees who are not on microphone so that everyone can hear the question and speakers have a moment to formulate a response. The moderator should reframe a question if it is on a tangential topic or off base and steer it to a specific speaker who has particular expertise on the issue or who has not been as involved in the discussion.

Interrupting

Effective moderators must be skilled at interrupting politely. Doing so is key to keeping the agenda on track when a speaker has gone on too long during opening remarks or when answering a question. Sometimes it is necessary when an attendee launches into longwinded remarks instead of asking a question. Interrupt kindly by waiting until the person speaking is taking a breath or ending a sentence. When necessary for online events, use the mute button on the videoconference platform. Thank the speaker and indicate what it is time to move on to, such as the next speaker or a new question from the audience.

Focusing Audience Attention in Virtual Formats

The facilitator can redirect the focus and attention of listeners in online panels and group presentations by spotlighting the panelist or presenter who is currently speaking. Also consider muting the sound and turning off the video feed for non-speaking panelists. If the panelists or speakers are engaged in frequent back-and-forth, then leaving the video and audio live makes perfect sense. Otherwise, use the tools of the videoconferencing platform to limit distractions and to help the audience focus on the active speaker.

Chapter 24

POSITIONING: PERSONAL INTRODUCTIONS AND ELEVATOR SPEECHES

Perhaps you have heard that you should have a minute long "elevator speech" ready in case you serendipitously hop on an elevator with the leader of the organization where you have always wanted to work or the key investor you have been pursuing to help you get a new venture off the ground. Maybe you have given some thought to how you would introduce yourself if you ever have that once-in-a-lifetime chance encounter in an elevator. But, if you are like many professionals, you assume you will never be in that sort of situation, so you haven't worried about preparing an elevator speech.

You are probably right about never needing to pitch yourself in an elevator. However, you will certainly need to introduce yourself at networking events, conferences, social functions, and even job interviews—anywhere you are asked "Tell me about yourself" or "What do you do?" If you are not approaching these situations as opportunities to give a strategic introduction of yourself, you are missing opportunities to grow both professionally and personally.

Just because you are introducing yourself in a conversational or small group setting, it does not mean you should wing it. In fact, you should prepare and rehearse your elevator speech with the care you would give a presentation to a large audience.

Prepare and rehearse your elevator speech with the care you would give a presentation to a large audience.

Similar to our approach to public speaking throughout this book, your goal should not be a scripted and unchanging set of remarks that is committed to memory. Instead, approach your personal introduction by analyzing and adapting to the audience and occasion (see chapter 3), crafting an outline, rehearsing until you can internalize key ideas and be conversational (see chapter 17), and receiving feedback and reworking material if you are not achieving the results you want. This chapter will provide guidance on crafting the key elements of a memorable elevator speech or personal introduction.

Start Strong

The most important part of your elevator speech is the first sentence. Your opening line is typically when you feel the most nervous and have the greatest tendency to stammer. This is also the point when people you meet are making judgments based on first impressions. It is important to have a pre-planned opening line that draws your listener in—just like you would for a speech.

When you don't have much time, this sentence becomes the abridged version of your elevator speech. And even when you do have a minute or two for the extended version of your personal introduction, the first sentence will determine whether the person or people you are talking to will continue to listen or if they will tune you out.

For that important first sentence, describe yourself as a solution to a problem faced by your clients, customers, or colleagues. Listeners don't necessarily care what your job title is, the certifications you have, or how your industry describes the work you do. They want to know how you can help them solve a problem. Here are some examples:

- "I'm an accountant at ACME Accounting who takes the dread out of April 15."

- "I'm an architect who breathes new life into historic buildings by making them more functional and efficient while preserving their character and charm."

- "I'm a tax-policy expert who promotes justice and equity through updates to our state's tax code."

- "I'm an attorney who demystifies and streamlines the patent process for life scientists who make breakthrough discoveries."

Remember, when you are introducing yourself, you must craft the first line of your elevator speech to provide them the answer to the age-old question, "What's in it for me?" Getting to the bottom line in plain terms will ensure listeners engage with you and that their eyes don't glaze over as you recite your official title, certifications, or other jargon.

If you are an early-career professional, you may not have developed the expertise to describe yourself as a solution to a problem. Or perhaps you are looking to make a career change and need to focus on where you want your career to go. In that case, use the first sentence of your introduction to give a brief overview of your past, your present, and your future goals. For example:

- "I recently finished my second year of law school at Willamette University, I'm currently a summer associate in the media and entertainment law practice group at Acme Law Firm, and I'm interested in cases related to journalists' privilege under the First Amendment."

- "I started my career as an IT specialist; I have now served as a systems administrator for 10 years; and I'm looking for a c-suite role in information security at a financial-services firm."

Admittedly, it is difficult to distill all your professional activities to a short statement. Remember, this sentence is meant to start a dialogue and is not a stand-in for your entire resume. It is important to simplify and focus on an area of your work that is most interesting to you and relevant to your audience. The opening line can and should change—it will include more detail if you are networking at an industry conference than it will at a happy hour hosted by your alma mater.

To get started, brainstorm three different ways you could craft the first line of your elevator speech. Share your drafted opening lines with three trusted colleagues, classmates, or friends. Which opening line resonated with them most? Why? How could you make that line more compelling so that it would be memorable and spur conversation?

Tell an Anecdote

After you describe how you solve a problem for the people you work with or give an overview of your past, present, and future, tell a short story to explain your motivation for doing what you do or highlighting a key success. This anecdote should be a "signature story"—one that reveals the ah-ha moment when you realized you wanted to do what you do or an example that reveals how exceptional you are at your craft.

The value of telling an anecdote is that people enjoy stories (it is the reason we stay up until the wee hours reading a page turner or binging on streaming TV shows), they are more memorable than highlights from a resume (people at networking events don't always remember a name, but they can recount an interesting narrative), they are easy to tell dynamically (you likely have shared signature stories many times before and enjoy telling them), and they build rapport with listeners (opening up by sharing a personal story can help establish a connection even with someone you just met).

Remember that your anecdote must be brief—your entire elevator speech should be just one to two minutes long. It should have a few specific details and vivid language to make the story interesting, colorful, concrete, and memorable.

Start a Dialogue

Finally, end with an open-ended question—one that cannot be answered with a simple "yes" or "no." The goal of an elevator speech is not to give a speech, but to start a conversation. Shift from a monologue to a dialogue. After all, you can't learn about someone you just met while your lips are moving. You have to let your ears do the work.

> *The goal of an elevator speech is not to give a speech, but to start a conversation.*

The question you ask at the end of your introduction can be as simple as, "And what is it that you do?" or "What's the most interesting thing you've learned at this conference?" Depending on the occasion, you can make it more specific to the event, your field of work, or the type of person you are networking with: "Does your company do work on historic buildings?" or "What type of law do you practice?"

More than anything else, your question must show you are interested in learning more about the person you are meeting. As you continue to converse, ask questions that spark interest in the person you are speaking with. Try to quickly find a topic they are passionate about. You will know you found the right topic when you observe their eyebrows go up, a sparkle in their eyes, variations in their voice, and energy in their body language. This may not be a work topic for every person you meet in professional situations. Family, hobbies, sports, and travel are good bets if work-related questions are falling flat.

Have realistic expectations for your personal introduction. It is not likely that you will land a job or close a sale after giving your one-to-two-minute elevator speech or having a subsequent five-to-seven minute conversation at a networking event (a good rule of thumb for such interactions so you don't monopolize your conversational partner's time and vice versa). You might have an enjoyable conversation that leads to an exchange of contact information, a follow-up email, and/or a connection on social media. That connection might lead to a lunch date, a meeting, a deeper conversation, and eventually, a professional relationship.

Like any part of presenting, being a good listener can pay dividends. The next time you attend a networking event, pay attention to the introductions given by the new people you meet. Whose introduction was most interesting or memorable? Whose was boring or unintelligible? How did a person's introduction impact your conversation? What can you learn from your analysis of the introductions you encountered at the networking event that you can apply to your own personal introduction/elevator speech?

The term elevator speech may be ill-suited because you likely will never have to pitch someone in an elevator, and the goal is not to give a speech but to start a conversation that can lead to a deeper connection over time. However, the formula for a successful personal introduction is far less tricky: start strong by positioning yourself as a solution to a problem or overviewing your past, present, and future; share a personal anecdote that explains why you do what you do or demonstrates how good you are at it; and then, transform your introduction from a monologue to a dialogue. Make sure you prepare, rehearse, and regularly revisit your elevator speech to effectively market yourself and capitalize on opportunities that come your way—whether you are in an elevator or not!

HERE ARE A FEW QUESTIONS YOU CAN USE AT NETWORKING EVENTS TO START A CONVERSATION OR KEEP THE DIALOGUE GOING:

- This is a beautiful venue, have you been to an event here before?
- What made you decide to attend this event?
- How did you hear about this event?
- What would make this event successful for you?
- How did you end up in this line of work?
- What do you like most about your industry/company/job?
- What still surprises you about your work/your industry?
- What do you wish people outside your line of work knew about it?
- How do you spend your time?
- What goals are you pursuing now?

Elevator Speech Examples

Example 1:

I'm Christine Clapp, the founder and president of Spoken with Authority where we elevate the presence and expand the influence of subject-matter experts, emerging leaders, and leaders. When I was a college freshman, I had to participate in debate as a requirement of my major. After losing all of my first 12 debates, I dedicated myself to improving my presentation skills. Not only did I qualify for the national tournament in my form of debate by the end of my sophomore year, I debated regionally, nationally, and internationally, making it to the World Universities Debating Championship my senior year of college. By the time I graduated college, I knew my life's work would be empowering others with communication skills. Do you know anyone who struggles with public speaking?

Example 2:

If you are an early-career professional or more seasoned professional who is changing fields, you may find it difficult to describe yourself as a solution to a problem. Consider discussing your past, present, and future:

> *I'm Tamika Jones. I recently finished my second year of law school at Willamette University, I'm currently a summer associate in the media and entertainment law practice group at Acme Law Firm, and I'm interested in cases related to journalists' privilege under the First Amendment. What areas of law do you practice?*

Chapter 25

INTERVIEWING: FOR JOBS AND PROMOTIONS

The U.S. Bureau of Labor Statistics reported that Americans have worked for their current employer an average of 4.1 years.[1] This number has been declining and the pandemic has accelerated the acceptance of short tenures with an employer.

If you are reading this chapter, you may be in the process of interviewing for a position or promotion—or you may be sooner than you think. It is time to rethink your interview strategy. Approach it as an opportunity to sell who you are, not what you know.

> *Approach a job interview as an opportunity to sell who you are, not what you know.*

Reject Conventional Wisdom

Conventional wisdom declares the purpose of a job interview is to elaborate on qualifications—what you know. But employers do not waste time interviewing candidates who do not meet basic requirements. They use your resume to make this judgment.

In the vast majority of cases, you are already deemed qualified when you are asked for a phone, online, or in-person interview. The interview, then, is really about finding out if you are a good fit in terms of personality.

BEHAVIORAL INTERVIEW QUESTIONS

Common in job interviews, behavioral interview questions give interviewers a concrete example of how you acted in the past so they can better understand how you will act in a similar situation in the future. This information is valuable to recruiters because humans are more likely to act similarly to how they behaved in the past than to respond as they say they would in a hypothetical situation. Here are examples of such prompts:

- Describe a time when you successfully dealt with an angry customer.

- What is a leadership role you have held?

- Tell me about a time you had to raise an uncomfortable issue with your boss.

- When did you make a mistake and how did you correct it?

- Share an example of a goal and how you achieved it.

- Describe a project you brought to completion and your role in it.

Job-interview experts recommend using the STAR Method for responding to behavioral interview questions. "S" stands for the situation; "T" for task; "A" for action; and "R" for result. Your responses should describe a situation you were in or the task you were assigned, the action you took, and the results you achieved.

The STAR Method is a powerful strategy to structure the 12 stories this chapter advises you to brainstorm and rehearse for your interview. A main benefit of using this format for each story is that it reminds interviewees to emphasize results. The result or outcome is something many interviewees forget to mention or quantify. Utilizing the STAR Method is a powerful and easy-to-remember strategy to structure the stories you share in job interviews.

Identify Key Strengths

Come up with three adjectives that you want the interviewer to associate with you. These qualities should position you as a good fit for the job and provide insights into your unique qualities as a person. Interviewers hear from many candidates who say they are hard workers, team players, and fast learners, but they likely do not hear from many candidates who say they are competitive, resilient, or observant. If you have a competitive spirit and having the drive to win is an asset in the position you're interviewing for, then it should be one of the themes you go back to in the stories you share during your interview. The same idea goes for resiliency or perceptiveness.

The point is that you should avoid common, trite, or "stock" responses that many candidates will give about their personal traits or strengths. Stand out from the crowd and strategically identify some unique traits about yourself that could be an asset in the position and for the organization. It is better to be rejected for being authentic and different, rather than boring, safe, and indistinguishable from other eager candidates.

Identify Key Experiences

Next, think of at least three important experiences in your life that have shaped who you are. Such experiences might include your hometown or state, sports you played growing up, family, schools you attended, languages you speak, volunteer work you enjoyed, jobs you have held in the past, hobbies, or travel. Remember not to limit yourself to paid employment. Formative experiences often happen outside the office and should be discussed in a job interview.

There is a good chance that many important life experiences you identify are missing from your resume or would take an extremely careful reading to tease out. You should not leave it up to the interviewer to read between the lines of your resume to figure out who you are and what you value.

Some job seekers might consider their religion, caregiving status, or a disability to be one of their key life experiences, but question whether they should bring it up in an interview. This is an intensely personal choice and there is no one-size-fits-all answer. Your decision to disclose and discuss these types of details of your life may open you up to discrimination—either in the interview process or if you land the job. Though illegal, this discrimination still happens.

Unless you are between jobs and desperate for a paycheck, being honest about who you are in the job interview will improve the chances that you will be happy and productive in your next position. It may be Pollyanna, but our hope is that more and more organizations accept, embrace, and celebrate candidates from diverse backgrounds and historically marginalized groups.

Brainstorm Stories

Once you have identified your key strengths and experiences, brainstorm a dozen specific stories from your work and personal life that highlight them. These stories provide the "evidence" for your traits and an opportunity to mention key life experiences. You will use this inventory of narratives to respond to behavioral interview questions (see sidebar for more on this type of question) as well as other common questions, such as "What is your greatest strength?" "Why do you want this job?" and "Tell me about a time you held a leadership position." (See chapter 24 for guidance on answering "Tell me about yourself.")

> *Stories provide the "evidence" for your traits and an opportunity to mention key life experiences.*

If asked directly in an interview what your greatest strengths are and what experiences have shaped you, you certainly could rattle off the list of three traits and three or more experiences you identified. But your responses will be more believable and memorable if you tell several stories that highlight those traits and experiences rather than recalling a list of adjectives and experiences that have no context.

It requires practice and discipline to bridge, or artfully segue, the question an interviewer asks to a story you want to tell. You should not only practice saying your 12 stories aloud multiple times with a focus on mentioning the specific key traits you identified, you should also conduct a mock interview or two with a friend or coach so you develop the habit of transitioning from the question asked to a story you want to answer. Work on linking the question to the story you want to tell. For example, "I'm glad you asked about a leadership position I've held. While I could tell you about leading a team of six project managers in my current position, I'd like to tell you about the success I had as the president of the Acme Toastmasters Club, which isn't listed on my resume but a great example of resilience." (See more on impromptu speaking in chapter 18.) Record and review your mock interview to assess not only the quality of your bridging and storytelling, but also your delivery. (See chapter 10 for an overview of the six elements of executive presence and authenticity.)

The goal of rehearsing is to confidently and conversationally control the message with your responses to interview questions such that at the end of the interview, the person or people interviewing you have written in their notes your key traits and life experiences and will remember a few of the stories you told to highlight those traits and experiences. You will not be able to relate every question to a rehearsed story, especially in the case of future-looking questions like "Where do you see yourself in five years?" and "What types of projects would you like to work on if you join our team?" The overall aim is to be prepared to share these stories for the bulk of behavioral interview questions you are asked.

Prepare for Problems

Job candidates are increasingly asked to conduct interviews by videoconference, to deliver a presentation with slides as part of the interview, or to record and upload answers to a series of interview questions on a computer-mediated platform. In these situations, remember the job interview is not about the technology, but the medium (and the problems it creates) can reveal the character of an applicant. Realize that managers and hiring committees are interpreting how you manage tech problems that arise during the interview process as evidence of who you are. Prepare yourself to demonstrate your key strengths when anticipating, preventing, and managing issues. In addition to mentally preparing, there are additional setup matters you can consider (but be sure to see chapter 16 on setup).

Professionals are interviewing for jobs and promotions more frequently than ever before. You can improve your performance and the likelihood of landing your ideal job by selling what you know on your resume; selling who you are in the job interview; identifying unique traits that position you as a good fit for the job; bridging questions to stories that bolster your claims about who you are and highlight key life experiences; and proactively avoiding technical problems and seamlessly switching to a back-up plan when they do arise.

ACE A COMPUTER MEDIATED JOB INTERVIEW

Laura Labovich, a national job search expert and chief executive officer of The Career Strategy Group, a boutique outplacement firm in Washington D.C., offers the following advice to job seekers who are interviewing on a videoconference platform:

- Unlike virtual presentations, which are ideally half the length of an in-person presentation, job interviews are not typically shorter when conducted online. Set aside two hours, just in case.

- Despite interviewing from the comfort of home, interviewees must still prepare for the interview as if it were held in person. Ideally, this includes recording and practicing a virtual interview with a friend or coach and reviewing the video to spot distracting behaviors and areas for improvement.

- Your background is an extension of your clothing. Consider it an outfit accessory, such as a tie or necklace. The background should complement the color and style of your clothing and never detract from your professionalism. Avoid preloaded virtual backgrounds. Test your setting during a practice virtual interview so you know exactly how it will appear on camera. (See more on setup in chapter 16.)

- It is still a job interview even if held online. Wear a full suit or what you would wear for an in-person interview.

- Join the videoconference three to five minutes before your interview start time. Some recruiters use the same videoconference link for many interviews; if you dial in too early, you might inadvertently interrupt another interview if the organizer did not enable a virtual waiting room.

- Ask the interviewer for a phone number to call if the videoconference technology fails during your interview.

- When speaking and not taking notes, look directly into the camera lens on your computer to you give the interviewer the experience of direct eye contact. (See chapter 15 for more on effective eye contact.)

- Have a printed cheat sheet with key stories and examples, as well as questions about the position and process. Keep it off camera but tell the interviewer early in the interview that you have notes. You might say: "If you see me glance down, it's because I captured some key information in my notes that I wanted to make sure I shared with you today."

- Take notes during the interview that you can use as fodder for your follow-up communication. The follow-up should be a carefully crafted influence letter and not a perfunctory thank-you. If you only have one computer monitor, split it so that half is a Word document for your notes and the other half is the videoconference platform.

- Make sure you send your follow-up communication via hard copy and by e-mail (in case the recruiter is working remotely, or the snail mail is slow).

Notes:

1. U.S. Bureau of Labor Statistics, "Employee Tenure Survey," September 22, 2020, https://bit.ly/3PzRyV9

Chapter 26

CELEBRATING: TOASTS AND AWARD ACCEPTANCE SPEECHES

Celebratory speeches can be some of the most important and difficult to give because they require us to articulate feelings about people we love or causes we are passionate about. Counterintuitively, they are also the presentations that speakers often, and unsuccessfully, try to deliver without preparation.

You may possibly remember hearing a toast at a wedding or retirement party that did not hit the right notes. Perhaps it contained insides jokes or embarrassing information about the person it was meant to honor. You might also remember Sally Field's often-mocked acceptance speech from March 1985 for her second Oscar for Best Actress based on her role in the film *Places in the Heart*. It ended with the following lines:

> *This means so much more to me this time, I don't know why. I think the first time I hardly felt it because it was all so new. But I want to say thank you to you. I haven't had an orthodox career. And I've wanted more than anything to have your respect. The first time I didn't feel it. But this time I feel it. And I can't deny the fact that you like me, right now, you like me!*

This chapter aims to help speakers who give toasts and those who give and receive awards to deliver remarks that rise to special occasions and will be remembered for all the right reasons.

Prepare Remarks

On rare occasions, award recipients are not aware that they are being considered for an award and they are forced to give an impromptu acceptance speech. Most often, award recipients know ahead of time that they were nominated or selected for an honor. Hosts, close friends, and family members know that a retirement party, wedding, or special event is on the calendar. Impromptu speaking should not be used in these situations.

Some special occasions have more celebratory speeches than others. If you are unaware of event norms (cultural, organizational, etc.), ask. Except for winning an award you didn't know about, there is no excuse for an unprepared acceptance speech or toast. Listeners will expect a good measure of polish in your remarks, and you should seize the opportunity to plan and rehearse a speech that you won't regret later (either for being embarrassing or for overlooking an important thank-you).

> *Seize the opportunity to plan and rehearse a speech that you won't regret later.*

Although some believe it is bad luck to prepare remarks to accept an award for which one is nominated or unnecessary to prepare a toast that expresses heartfelt sentiments on a special occasion, it is far better to have prepared remarks that go unused than to wing your moment in the spotlight. Preparation requires more than scribbling a few words on a napkin just before you accept an award or give a toast. Approach it like any important presentation and start at least several days, and ideally, a few weeks in advance.

Give a Speech with a Message

This is a speech—not stand-up comedy or a laundry-list of thank-yous. Every speech has an introduction, body with a central idea, and a conclusion. Toasts and acceptance speeches are no exception.

While these types of speeches should include anecdotes, they should have a clear message that connects selected stories into a cohesive whole. That message may center on a quality you admire about a person or couple. It might be advice you have for the couple getting married or colleagues who will continue your work after you retire. The central idea for an award-acceptance speech may be related to the importance of the award, organization, industry, type of work, or your legacy.

You absolutely can and should include tasteful and humorous anecdotes in your speech. If it isn't possible or appropriate to explain a story or joke so that every guest can understand it, then it has no place in a toast or award acceptance speech. Leave that story for a personal conversation or correspondence. For toasts, check that the stories are about the person being honored and not the person giving the speech. It is easy to fall into the trap of focusing on how much the honoree means to you. While you can and should mention their importance, your toast should have relatively few references to "I" and "me." Also, be sure to balance entertaining stories with concrete advice and/or a poignant moral.

TIPS FOR TOASTS

A toast is just a speech if there isn't a drink at the end. Remember to invite other guests to join you in toasting the guest(s) of honor. You can say, "Please join me in raising a glass to . . ." or something as simple as "Cheers!"

Etiquette requires the host to give the first toast. You might be anxious to deliver your toast so you can continue celebrating, but wait for the host to kick things off.

Have a Hook

As mentioned above, toasts and acceptance speeches should have an introduction, one part of which is an attention-getting device. (See more about attention getters in chapter 7.) A wonderful example of a toast that begins with a catchy opening comes from the 2001 movie, *My First Mister*. The main character, Jennifer, a 17-year-old girl, begins a toast with the line, "I'd like to propose a toast to all the special 'f' words—to friends, family, fate, forgiveness, and forever." It's funny, sincere, memorable, and masterfully sets up the rest of the toast.

Many toasts and acceptance speeches start with a laundry-list of thank-yous. While thank-yous can come in the speech introduction, they should not be the first words out of your mouth. Take a cue from Jennifer in *My First Mister* and start with the interesting, compelling, funny, or memorable hook before you launch into thank-yous. For the introduction to a toast, be sure you also mention your relationship to the guest(s) of honor after the hook but still in the introduction of your speech.

Express Gratitude

Think ahead to identify all the people you should thank or otherwise recognize. It could be the host(s), attendees, guest(s) of honor, additional award winners, mentors, or others who made the event possible or contributed to your success. Do not miss out on an opportunity to show your gratitude publicly. It is acceptable to write down the list of people you would like to thank and refer to a small notecard (never notes written on your hand) as you mention them. Put the notecard away when you move on to the next section of your speech.

Be Concise

Think Hemingway, not Faulkner. Toasts and acceptance speeches should be short; two to three minutes is appropriate. If you are a dignitary, like the event host or lifetime award winner, you can stretch it to four or five minutes. It becomes uncomfortable when the speaker keeps talking over the play-off music. Even if your event does not play music to signal your time has expired, listeners will get restless if you go on too long.

Practice

Practice your planned speech at least six times aloud before the event so you can deliver it largely without notes and in an appropriate amount of time. It will not be memorized word for word, but your key points will be. If anything, you may want a small slip of paper or one notecard in your pocket with a few words or names written down to refer to if you are nervous, excited, or emotional and need the crutch. A conversational delivery (even with a few hiccups) will be a better fit for a party than the reading of a script.

If you do get emotional in the moment, don't worry. It is okay to cry, but you do not want to sob your way through the speech making it unintelligible. Stop speaking, glance down at your notes while you regain composure, and look back up at audience members when you are able to continue.

ADVICE FOR AWARD RECIPIENTS

When your name is called to accept an award, don't dilly-dally. You will have plenty of time to shake hands and hug friends after the ceremony.

When you get to the podium, approach the steps slowly and cautiously so you don't trip. Hold the award in your left hand and shake the presenter's hand with your right. Pause during the hand-shake, turning your body toward the audience and displaying the award so photographers can capture the moment.

Place the award on the lectern when possible so you don't distract listeners by fiddling or gesturing with it during your speech. Pause while the presenter is walking away from the lectern and audience members are concluding their applause. Smile and look out at the crowd before you start your acceptance speech.

Do not abuse your time in the spotlight. It can be tempting to use this occasion to raise awareness of a separate issue or to further your personal agenda. Be respectful of the organization giving you the award as well as the audience.

And at the conclusion of your acceptance speech, it is customary to stand at the lectern smiling until the emcee comes toward you to shake hands or you are escorted off the stage. Smile and embrace the audience applause graciously.

Speak Before Your Second Drink

On celebratory occasions when emotions may be running high, make sure you give your toast before you start your second drink. It might seem like a good idea to have a few drinks to calm your nerves, but it is not. Alcohol and public speaking do not mix well. Save yourself, the host, and guest(s) of honor potential embarrassment by sticking to water or speaking before you move on to your second adult drink.

Hold the Microphone Properly

Even the loudest voice is no match for a special event with guests mingling or eating. Plan to use a microphone. As you use it, be aware of microphone placement. If you hold it right up to your lips, you may get a muffled or garbled sound rather than a clear, amplified voice. If you hold it too low or too far in front of you, it might not pick up your voice.

Whenever possible, try to test the microphone during setup before the event to get familiar with proper microphone placement because each AV system is unique. Start by holding the microphone at a 45-degree angle several inches from your mouth (this is where you would hold an ice cream cone between licks) and adjust from there. Keep your chin up and speak with a strong voice. You might also discuss details of when speeches will be given during the celebration and where speakers should stand to avoid unpleasant audio feedback.

There will be plenty of opportunities to say a few words at special events like weddings, anniversaries, graduations, birthday parties, award ceremonies, and even celebrations of life. Do not make the mistake of staying silent or saying something unplanned that you later regret. Seize the opportunity of these special occasions to talk about who and what is most important to you by carefully preparing and practicing a short speech. Include stories and anecdotes to convey a poignant message or helpful advice to make the speech meaningful to everyone.

GUIDANCE FOR AWARD PRESENTERS

We generally recommend the extemporaneous mode of speaking because it promotes a conversational and dynamic delivery, but speakers who are presenting an award are well-served by writing out their remarks word-for-word. Scripting makes sense in situations when the presentation is short, and exactness of message is important.

When it comes to the content of the award presentation, make sure you provide an explanation of the award (what it is for and why it is important) as well as its history (how long it has been given and notable past recipients).

Then, pay tribute to the person being honored. You may include a few biographical details and mention key accomplishments. Keep this material brief so you can spend the bulk of your time sharing specific anecdotes and examples of the recipient's work that make them a worthy honoree.

Some award presenters withhold the recipient's name until the end of their presentation to add suspense. Others reveal the recipient's name early on. Either way is fine. Respect the tradition of the event and wishes of the event organizers before scripting your presentation. When naming the award winner, remember to identify and practice the correct pronunciation of the recipient's name, affiliations, and pronouns!

At the conclusion of the presentation of the award, you should welcome the recipient to the lectern. Begin by smiling warmly and leading audience members in applause. Avoid clapping into the microphone because it can hurt the ears of audience members.

As the recipient nears the lectern, take a few steps back from the lectern and a few steps in the direction of the award winner as you hold the award in both hands. When they are a few steps away, shift the award to your left hand and extend your right hand for a handshake. After pictures are taken, turn control of the award to the recipient and guide him or her to the lectern.

Move briskly to the side of or off the stage. You want to melt into the background as applause is winding down so your award recipient can take center stage.

Chapter 27

ENTERTAINING: AFTER DINNER SPEECHES

ow do you feel after dinner? More specifically, how do you feel after a dinner served in a banquet or ceremonial setting? Probably relaxed, maybe a little tired, hopefully gratified to be around excellent companions. This is the mood for most entertaining speeches, commonly referred to as an after-dinner speech.

As mentioned throughout this book, it is good to remember what it is like to be an audience member. It is also good to remember that you are not just an audience member when you are the speaker. The balance between the informality of the moment and formality of being the one speaking is key to effective after-dinner speaking. The considerations we offer below will help you to rise to the occasion and entertain an audience.

The Sentiment Should Be Light-Hearted

As you consider what to say, do not burden yourself with trying to be profound or deeply moving. Have a point, and perhaps even a persuasive one, but keep it light. If a moment of seriousness or solemnity is necessary, try to situate that in the middle of your remarks.

Be Entertaining in a Way That Makes Sense to You

Many after-dinner speeches are humorous, but don't feel pressured to play the role of a comedian. Entertainment can happen with stories, anecdotes, hypotheticals, and vivid description.

It does not have to be jokes. And if you do tell jokes, be mindful of their appropriateness. It is easy to get caught up in the moment—everyone seems relaxed and is having an enjoyable time, so you decide to push the boundary and tell an embarrassing story about a co-worker or an off-color joke. Just remember, you can't take it back once you say it. Also, no one ever got fired for not telling a joke, but plenty of people have experienced the negative repercussions of being inappropriate.

Be Wary of Improvisation

For all of the above reasons, it is important to prepare your remarks and avoid improvisation, or "winging it." This does not mean that you need to create a manuscript and commit it to memory. It means that you should draft your Sandwich Structure outline and practice it. (See chapter 5 on outlining and chapter 17 on rehearsing.) The looseness of the moment should come through in your tone and facial expressions, not in your lack of content and structure. Your comfort and ease in the presentation will help bring the entertaining elements to the presentation.

The Structure of an After-Dinner Speech Can Be Subtle

Your goal for this speech is to contribute to the mood more than it is to persuade listeners to your position or to inform audience members about a specific topic. Because data retention is not a primary goal, after-dinner speeches often have subtle previews and transitions in place of the more direct signposting that you would use in an informative briefing or persuasive presentation. Having structure, albeit subtle, that brings meaningful movement to the content will keep the audience engaged and make the presentation easier for you to present.

Do Not Expect an Attentive Audience

Audience members may be finishing their meal, finding the restroom, or even conversing with nearby dining mates. If you are in a banquet room, you will be speaking over servers clearing plates, refilling drinks, and circulating throughout the room. Do not allow the distractions to frustrate you. Expect them—they are just part of the context. In your preparation, include a few clear statements that express the sentiment you are trying to achieve. Repetition, directness, and simplicity will help ensure listeners get the main idea despite the distractions.

After-dinner speeches and dessert share many characteristics. They both mark the end of the meal, they both should be enjoyable, and you should avoid having too much of either. If you understand the expectations for the occasion and play to your own strengths, your speech, much like an excellent dessert, will be delightful.

PRACTICE WITH DISTRACTIONS

In preparation for an entertaining speech, practice your presentation with the television on. If you can remain focused while managing the distractions, you will be better able to manage disruptions during an after-dinner speech.

Chapter 28

INSPIRING: KEYNOTE SPEECHES, COMMENCEMENT ADDRESSES, AND TED-STYLE TALKS

In the film *Remember the Titans*, Coach Herman Boone (played by Denzel Washington) delivers a rousing speech in an attempt to unite his racially divided high school football team. Washington is a highly regarded actor who has won Academy Awards for both Best Actor (2001) and Best Supporting Actor (1989), and in that onscreen speech, we can see why.

Delivering a motivational speech in the real world is not the same. We are not Denzel Washington, nor do we get the benefit of multiple takes. It would be a mistake to try to reproduce the inspirational speeches from films like *Remember the Titans*, *Hoosiers*, *Braveheart*, or *Invictus*. How then, can we mere mortals craft inspirational speeches that can move listeners?

One example is the May 9, 2022, commencement address delivered by Rollins College's Valedictorian Elizabeth Bonker that centered on the theme of "Life is for service." The moving six-minute speech, delivered with text-to-speech software (Bonker is affected by nonspeaking autism) demonstrates six key components of inspirational speeches—whether they are delivered at a graduation, for a conference keynote, or on a TED or TEDx stage.

Be Authentic

It is somewhat odd to say "Be yourself" when discussing the act of public speaking. For most people, being yourself would include not giving public speeches! That said, it is important to avoid acting like someone else. Do not play a character—audiences recognize when you are disingenuous. Early in her address, Bonker acknowledged "I am affected by a form of autism that doesn't allow me to speak. My neuromotor issues also prevent me from tying my shoes or buttoning a shirt without assistance. I have typed this speech with one finger with a communication partner holding a keyboard." She exemplifies honesty and authenticity.

Make the Sentiment Clear

Like all ceremonial speeches, it is important that a speech to inspire is sentimentally definitive. This means that if your purpose is to inspire, then the speech should avoid too much discussion of challenges or negativity. Also, have a clear point. Listeners should leave with a moral like "family is important," or "hard work will pay off." In the case of Bonker's speech, it is "Life is for service," a phrase famous Rollins alumnus Mister Rogers is credited with having written on a note that he kept in his wallet. Your main idea need not be as specific or as explicitly stated as it would be in a how-to speech, training program, or sales pitch, but it must be present and conveyed to listeners.

Build to Your Point

An inspirational speech does not need to reach saccharine highs, but it does need to build toward a point. In doing this, you can certainly discuss challenges and hardships. Generally, discussion of obstacles is best placed at either the beginning or the middle of the presentation. If placed at the beginning, you can build toward the inspirational point; if placed in the middle, you are able to begin and end on more positive notes.

In the passage quoted from the introduction of her speech, Bonker did mention specific struggles she faced, but at the halfway point in her address she delved deeper, "Personally, I have struggled my whole life with not being heard or accepted. A story on the front page of our local newspaper reported how the principal at my high school told a staff member, 'The [R-word] can't be valedictorian.'" She immediately pivoted to a positive point, "Yet today, here I stand. Each day, I choose to celebrate small victories, and today, I am celebrating a big victory with all of you."

Tell Stories

Inspirational speakers often rely on stories, rather than facts or statistics, to support their message. Just make sure that you, the presenter, aren't always the hero in the stories told. True, personal narratives, like the one Bonker shared about the quotation in the local newspaper, can lend credibility and increase connection with listeners. Taken to the extreme, they can have the opposite effect and come across as self-congratulatory. Bonker effectively balanced sharing personal stories with anecdotes about classmates committed to service, as well as quotations from well-known authors.

In graduation addresses, stories often move from "I" (meaning the speaker) to "we" (meaning the graduates) to "us" (meaning a part of society or the global community). They also often simultaneously progress from the past to the present to the future. Another way to think about storytelling in inspirational speeches comes from Nancy Duarte's book *Resonate*. She uses a *Star Wars* metaphor and recommends that speakers leverage narratives that put themselves in the Yoda/adviser role and cast audience members in the Luke Skywalker/hero role.

Involve Your Audience

Inspiring an audience involves emotionally moving an audience. They might be moved to act or moved to think, but you are trying to move them. To that end, you should make explicit appeals to audience members (most often in the conclusion of an inspiration speech). Concretely describe how listeners achieve the principles or goals you discuss. Make sure this question does not go unanswered, or else your motivational message will fall flat.

Bonker's commencement address includes a masterful call to action, most common in persuasive speeches, although persuasion often is a secondary purpose of inspirational speeches (see more on persuasion and calls to action in chapter 22). Here's what Bonker said, "So, my call to action today is simple. Tear off a small piece from your commencement program and write 'Life is for Service' on it. Yes. We gave you the pens to really do it. Let's start a new tradition. Take a photo and post it on social media. Then put it in your wallet or some other safe place, just as Mister Rogers did. And when we see each other at our reunions, we can talk about how our commencement notes reminded us to serve others."

Clinch Confidently

Clinching speeches is always important, but it is even more important for a speech where your intent is to motivate. Without a confident ending, all of the hard work that you have done in the speech will be minimized. (See chapter 7 for more on effective clinchers.)

To conclude, Bonker shares a quotation bringing full circle the challenges from her introduction (those that made many dismiss her and devalue her humanity) to the clincher. The quotation serves as a clincher to inspire her classmates to reach beyond what is expected of them: "My fellow classmates, I leave you today with a quote from Alan Turing, who broke the Nazi encryption code to help win World War II. 'Sometimes, it is the people no one imagines anything of who do the things no one can imagine.' Be those people. Be the light! Fiat lux. Thank you."

You may never give an inspirational speech at an important sporting event or on a battlefield, but you may find yourself serving as a speaker for a conference keynote, at a commencement ceremony, as part of a TED or TED-style event, or as the leader of a team that has experienced a loss, setback, or seemingly insurmountable challenge. These moments require much of presenters. Keep in mind the six important components to successful inspirational speaking as well as principles of persuasion. Remember that speeches to inspire require additional preparation time and may benefit from a scripted and thoroughly rehearsed or even memorized delivery. Considering these factors will provide you the confidence to speak up at these pivotal times and discover a winning formula for your specific purpose, audience, and occasion.

STYLISTIC DEVICES TO MOVE YOUR AUDIENCE

There are many stylistic devices to consider incorporating to help move your audience. Here are a few:

Isocolon is a scheme of parallel structure that occurs when the parallel elements are similar not only in grammatical structure but also in length (number of words, or even number of syllables).

> **Example:** His purpose was to impress the ignorant, to perplex the dubious, and to confound the scrupulous.

Antithesis is the juxtaposition of contrasting ideas, often in parallel structure. The contrast may be in words or in ideas or both.

> **Example:** What if I am rich, and another is poor; strong, and he is weak; intelligent, and he is benighted; elevated, and he is depraved? Have we not one Father? Hath not one God created us? – William Lloyd Garrison, "No Compromise with Slavery."

Anaphora is the repetition of the same word or groups of words at the beginnings of successive clauses. This device produces a strong emotional effect, especially in speech. It also establishes a marked change in rhythm.

> **Example:** Why should white people be running all the stores in our community? Why should white people be running the banks of our community? Why should the economy of our community be in the hands of the white man? Why? – Malcolm X.

Climax is the arrangement of words, phrases, or clauses in an order of increasing importance.

> **Example:** More than that, we rejoice in our sufferings, knowing that suffering produces endurance, endurance produces character, and character produces hope, and hope does not disappoint us, because God's love has been poured into our hearts through the Holy Spirit which has been given to us. – Paul to the Romans.

Chiasmus is the repetition of words in successive clauses in reverse syntactic order.

> **Example:** Ask not what your country can do for you; ask what you can do for your country. – John F. Kennedy, Inaugural address.

Antanaclasis is the repetition of a word in two different senses.

> **Example:** Your argument is sound, nothing but sound. – Benjamin Franklin.

> **Example:** If we don't hang together, we'll hang separately. – Benjamin Franklin.

Hyperbole is exaggeration for the purpose of emphasis or heightened effect.

> **Example:** I nearly died I was so embarrassed.

Litotes is the deliberate use of understatement.

Example: It isn't very serious. I have this tiny little tumor on the brain. – JD Salinger, The Catcher in the Rye

Paradox is an apparent contradictory statement that nevertheless contains some measure of truth.

Example: Art is a form of lying in order to tell the truth. – Pablo Picasso

Paralepsis is emphasizing something by seemingly passing over it.

Example: I refuse to talk about my opponents multiple failed marriages. That is not what this campaign is about.

Hypophora is asking questions then immediately answering them.

Example: Can we provide better service? Yes. Can we save you money? Yes. Will you become a member of ABC Credit Union? We hope you say yes.

Final Thoughts

FORETHOUGHTS FOR FUTURE SUCCESS

Final thoughts are not very final. As we know all too well, the dynamics of professional presentations are constantly shifting and adapting to new exigencies in the working world. Contexts and norms evolve, sometimes slowly and sometimes quickly. For example, our first book, *Presenting at Work* (2016), focused mostly on in-person presentations because that was the norm. Our second book, *Presenting Virtually* (2020), addressed the dramatic shift to online modes of speaking necessitated by the COVID-19 pandemic. With this book, we add the hybrid experience into the mix, while still accounting for the important roles that in-person and online-only modes represent.

However, more modes of presentations should not mean more anxiety and uncertainty. Indeed, a little forethought can go a long way.

Forethought—the term is simple enough. Thought: meaning to consider, to analyze, to reflect. Fore: meaning in advance. Forethought, then, could be defined as considering matters in advance. We do this all the time, don't we?

Yes, absolutely. This concept has been a throughline in the advice dispensed in this book. The continuous practice of forethought, even when it seems obvious or inapplicable, can lead to greater confidence for you as a speaker.

One connotation of forethought is planning. We plan a presentation in advance. Much of this book provides useful protocols for elevating and streamlining this formal process of forethought. Asking "Why am I speaking to this audience on this occasion?" is one step in the process (see chapter 3). Using the Sandwich Structure to construct your presentation is another (see chapter 5). And developing useful and engaging presentation aids based on the Sandwich Structure is yet another (see chapter 9).

Forethought is also a commitment to developing your delivery skills. Delivery is not an oversized checklist that must be completed. It is instead an awareness of strengths and weaknesses (and we all have both). It is using the six S's as a shorthand vocabulary to be more purposeful and authentic with the fundamentals of delivery (see chapters 10 through 16). It is adopting strategies to reduce nervousness and remembering to practice six times (see chapters 2 and 17).

Forethought is remembering how you feel when you are an audience member, then using those insights to adapt your speaking. It is a simple but often overlooked strategy. As professionals with domain expertise, you might focus on content and forget about the experience of being an audience member. When you allow yourself this moment of reflection, you will ensure you have a clear introduction and conclusion (chapter 7). Similarly, you will clarify your signposting and transitions (chapter 8) so that your audience can follow your reasoning.

The flip side of this coin is to inquire how audience members who are not like you might receive your material. Part of this audience adaptation relates to content, but part of thinking about the audience includes accessibility and inclusion. (See chapter 1). The world continues to advance on matters of accessibility and inclusion, but the process is the same: stay curious and stay humble.

For us, part of the process of forethought has been thinking about the next frontier of presentations, such as virtual reality and augmented reality. The nuances between these and among other new technologies are less important to our point here than the fact that they are now and increasingly will become a part of the workplace communication landscape. With the dispersion of the workforce outside of a central office, these and other tools will provide options to move beyond the flatness of videoconferencing technology and provide new spaces for presenting, meeting, and learning. They may even lead to increased inclusion and understanding of neurodiverse individuals.[1]

Researchers are also developing computer-mediated experiences that allow neurotypical individuals to see the world as neurodivergent people experience it.[2] One of our mantras is that we aren't just training speakers, we're training listeners. By this we mean that many of the orthodoxies of public speaking came from, and benefit, a certain type of person who had the power to establish such norms. Empathy is critical in communication. Let's explore and embrace tools and technologies that will help expand our empathy.

These are just a few possibilities for the future of presentations and public speaking. If the early 2020s taught us anything, it is that you cannot anticipate everything. However, with forethought, built on a foundation of skills and strategies, we can adapt to challenges and seize the opportunities that lie ahead.

Notes:

1. For example, see William Jarrold, Peter Mundy, Mary Gwaltney, Jeremy Bailenson, Naomi Hatt, Nancy McIntyre, Kwanguk Kim, Marjorie Solomon, Stephanie Novotny, and Lindsay Swain, "Social Attention in a Virtual Public Speaking Task in Higher Functioning Children with Autism," *Autism Research* 6, no. 5 (2013): 393–410.

2. Greg Musser, "How Virtual Reality Is Transforming Autism Studies," *Spectrum*, October 24, 2018, https://bit.ly/3zYMvaU

Appendix I

SANDWICH STRUCTURES TEMPLATES

EXAMPLE

Chronological

Attention getter, relevance, credibility

Issue X is important

PREVIEW

T I. Past (history)	T II. Present (current developments)	T III. Future (outlook)
A.	A.	A.
B.	B.	B.
C.	C.	C.

REVIEW

Link to attention getter

EXAMPLE
Geographical

Attention getter, relevance, credibility

Issue X is impacting communities around the globe

PREVIEW

T I. Location A	T II. Location B	T III. Location C
A.	A.	A.
B.	B.	B.
C.	C.	C.

REVIEW

Link to attention getter

EXAMPLE
Monroe's Motivated Sequence

Attention getter, relevance, credibility

Reject this societal norm

PREVIEW

T I. **Need** (Problem)	T II. **Satisfaction** (Solution)	T III. **Visualization** (Benefits)
A.	A.	A.
B.	B.	B.
C.	C.	C.

REVIEW

Call to **action**

EXAMPLE

Three Story Structure

Attention getter, relevance, credibility

Support this cause

PREVIEW

T I. Success Story 1	T II. Success Story 2	T III. Success Story 3
A.	A.	A.
B.	B.	B.
C.	C.	C.

REVIEW

Link to attention getter / call to action

EXAMPLE

Process of Elimination

Attention getter, relevance, credibility

Options for moving forward

PREVIEW

T I. OPTION 1	T II. OPTION 2	T III. OPTION 3
A.	A.	A.
B.	B.	B.
C.	C.	C.

REVIEW

Next step should be #3 / call to action
Link to attention getter

Appendix II

ADDITIONAL RESOURCES ON PRESENTING AND SPEECH WRITING

Brothers, Chalmers, and Vinay Kumar. *Language and the Pursuit of Leadership Excellence: How Extraordinary Leaders Build Relationships, Shape Culture and Drive Breakthrough Results*. Naples: New Possibilities Press, 2015.

Cain, Susan. *Quiet: The Power of Introverts in a World That Can't Stop Talking*. New York: Crown, 2012.

Carnegie, Dale. *How to Win Friends & Influence People*. New York: Simon and Schuster, 1942.

Cialdini, Robert B. *Influence: The Psychology of Persuasion*. New York: Collins, 2007.

Clear, James. *Atomic Habits: An Easy & Proven Way to Build Good Habits & Break Bad Ones*. New York: Avery, 2018.

Cuddy, Amy. *Presence: Bringing Your Boldest Self to Your Biggest Challenges*. New Yor: Little Brown, 2015.

Duarte, Nancy. *Resonate: Present Visual Stories That Transform Audiences*. Hoboken, N.J.: Wiley, 2010.

Foer, Joshua. *Moonwalking with Einstein: The Art and Science of Remembering Everything*. New York: Penguin, 2011.

Genard, Gary. *Fearless Speaking: Beat Your Anxiety, Build Your Confidence, Change Your Life.* Arlington: Cedar & Maitland Press, 2014.

Goodwin, Doris Kearns. *Team of Rivals: The Political Genius of Abraham Lincoln.* New York: Simon and Schuster, 2005.

Heath, Chip, and Dan Heath. *Made to Stick: Why Some Ideas Survive and Others Die.* New York: Random House, 2007.

Heinrichs, Jay. *Thank You for Arguing: What Aristotle, Lincoln, and Homer Simpson Can Teach Us About the Art of Persuasion.* New York: Three Rivers Press, 2007.

Humes, James C. *Speak Like Churchill, Stand Like Lincoln: 21 Powerful Secrets of History's Greatest Speakers.* New York: Three Rivers Press, 2002.

Lanham, Richard A. *A Handlist of Rhetorical Terms: A Guide for Students of English Literature.* Berkeley: University of California Press, 1968.

Lehrman, Robert. *The Political Speechwriters' Companion: A Guide for Writers and Speakers.* Washington: CQ Press, 2009.

Lencioni, Patrick M. T*he Five Dysfunctions of a Team: Team Assessment.* San Francisco: Jossey-Bass, 2002.

Maxwell, John C., and John Maxwell. *The 360 Degree Leader.* Nashville, TN: Nelson, 2005.

Noonan, Peggy. *What I Saw At the Revolution: A Political Life in the Reagan Era.* New York: Random House, 1990.

Reynolds, Garr. *Presentation Zen: Simple Ideas on Presentation Design and Delivery.* 2nd ed. Berkeley, CA: New Riders, 2012.

Safire, William. *Lend Me Your Ears: Great Speeches in History.* Rev. and expanded ed. New York: W.W. Norton, 1997.

Sinek, Simon. *Start with Why: How Great Leaders Inspire Everyone to Take Action.* New York: Penguin, 2009.

Sorensen, Theodore C. *Counselor: A Life At the Edge of History.* New York, NY: Harper, 2008.

Van Edwards, Vanessa. *Captivate: The Science of Succeeding with People*. New York: Penguin, 2018.

Wills, Garry. *Lincoln At Gettysburg: The Words That Remade America*. New York: Simon & Schuster, 1992.

ABOUT THE AUTHORS

About Christine Clapp

Christine Clapp is the president of Spoken with Authority, a Washington, D.C.-based presentation skills consultancy that elevates the presence and expands the influence of professionals, and promotes inclusion in their organizations. Since 2008, Christine and her team of six presentation-skills experts have provided virtual and in-person training programs and coaching engagements to hundreds of organizations and thousands of leaders, emerging leaders, and subject-matter experts. She holds two degrees in communication: a bachelor's degree from Willamette University, and a master's degree from the University of Maryland, College Park. Christine also taught public speaking to undergraduate and graduate students at the George Washington University for thirteen years.

About Bjørn F. Stillion Southard

Bjørn F. Stillion Southard is an Associate Professor of Communication Studies at the University of Georgia, where he teaches and researches on the history of public speaking in the United States. At the University, Bjørn teaches courses on argumentation, public speaking, and American oratory. He researches on the subject of race and public address, publishing numerous academic journal articles and book chapters, as well as an award-winning book on the subject. Bjørn has taught thousands of students and worked with hundreds of clients on the art and craft of public speaking. He received his PhD and MA in Communication from the University of Maryland, College Park, and his BA in Rhetoric and Media Studies from Willamette University.

About Both Authors

Christine Clapp and Bjørn F. Stillion Southard were debate partners as undergraduate students at Willamette University and their graduate schooling overlapped at the University of Maryland, College Park. They authored two other books together, *Presenting Virtually: A Guide to Public Speaking in Online Contexts* (2020) and *Presenting at Work: A Guide to Public Speaking in Professional Contexts* (2014). They also are collaborators with David Henderson on *Let 'Em Speak,* a podcast launched in 2020 about the risks and rewards of real talk by real people in the real world, and through their work at Spoken with Authority.

Presenting Now aims to take advantage of the extraordinary opportunity to reinvent post-pandemic communication, both online and in-person, in ways that are more flexible, authentic, engaging, equitable, and sustainable. Created for busy, results-oriented professionals, this new book is loaded with potent and practical tools, methods, and insights that will help you:

Thanks for your interest in *Presenting Now!* Please consider leaving a review for our book on Amazon!

LET'S STAY IN TOUCH!

https://spokenwithauthority.com

info@spokenwithauthority.com

https://twitter.com/SpokenAuthority

https://www.linkedin.com/company/spoken-with-authority

Made in the USA
Middletown, DE
04 November 2023

41822041R00137